Moving the Stars With Your Words

How to be the creative factor & achieve what you really want out of life

by

Harold Davis, Msc.D., Ph.D

Moving The Stars Seminars, Inc.
237 Tramway Dr, Suite B, Box 4470
Lake Tahoe, NV 89449
(775)588-6418
(866)200-5174
E-mail: mts@movingthestars.com
Web site: www.MovingTheStars.com

© Copyright 2004 Dr. Harold Davis, Msc.D. Ph.D. All rights reserved.

No part of this publication may be reproduced, stored in a retrieval system, or transmitted, in any form or by any means, electronic, mechanical, photocopying, recording, or otherwise, without the written prior permission of the author.

Printed in Victoria, Canada

Cover Design by David Jacobs
www.anthemmg.com

Moving The Stars Seminars, Inc.
237 Tramway Dr., Suite B, Box 4470
Lake Tahoe, NV 89449
(775)588-6418
(866)200-5174
E-mail: mts@movingthestars.com
Web site: www.MovingTheStars.com

National Library of Canada Cataloguing in Publication Data

A cataloguing record for this book that includes the U.S. Library of Congress Classification number, the Library of Congress Call number and the Dewey Decimal cataloguing code is available from the National Library of Canada. The complete cataloguing record can be obtained from the National Library's online database at: www.nlc-bnc.ca/amicus/index-e.html

ISBN 1-4120-2772-1

TRAFFORD

This book was published *on-demand* in cooperation with Trafford Publishing.
On-demand publishing is a unique process and service of making a book available for retail sale to the public taking advantage of on-demand manufacturing and Internet marketing.
On-demand publishing includes promotions, retail sales, manufacturing, order fulfilment, accounting and collecting royalties on behalf of the author.

Suite 6E, 2333 Government St., Victoria, B.C. V8T 4P4, CANADA
Phone	250-383-6864	Toll-free	1-888-232-4444 (Canada & US)
Fax	250-383-6804	E-mail	sales@trafford.com
Web site	www.trafford.com	TRAFFORD PUBLISHING IS A DIVISION OF TRAFFORD HOLDINGS LTD.	
Trafford Catalogue #04-0600		www.trafford.com/robots/04-0600.html	

10   9   8   7   6   5   4   3

Foreword
by Jeffery Combs

Author of More Heart Than Talent

I have had the good fortune of knowing Harold Davis for over five years in a number of different capacities. He has been a dedicated student, an entrepreneur, a life coach, a speaker, an athlete, and now a writer.

His approach and philosophy toward life have allowed hundreds of people to choose the experiences they desire to have, and from there, to literally speak those experiences into existence.

Harold definitely understands the word commitment, having been an All-American runner in track and field while in college, then taking that dedication to Corporate America and now Free Enterprise. Harold speaks direct from his heart and knows that your words and your thought forms are your law. Harold Davis is the leader you are looking for!

- *Jeffery Combs,*
  President of Golden Mastermind Seminars, Inc.
  www.GoldenMastermind.com

What Successful People Are Saying About Moving the Stars With Your Words

"Harold has captured the spiritual essence of the power of our words to create the life we desire to live, this book is a must read"
-*Chaneta Lewis & Evelyn Coulson*
Co-founders of Core Essence
www.Coressence.net

"Harold has developed a life strategy that will change your life in a very powerful way"
-*Brian Wirth,*
Executive Director, TriVita Way Corporation

"This book is a highly effective tool that will assist you in creating a winning pattern for your life"
-*Rene' Dickerson, RN*
Founder, Healthy Balance Now
www.HealthyBalanceNow.com

"What an awesome practical guide, providing insights into everyday issues we all have and are trying to deal with. I can honestly say after reading, "Moving the Stars With Your Words" that many of life's issues are all in the mind and only you have the power to make a meaningful change"
-*Horace U. Grant, MBA*
School Business Manager
Houston Independent School District

"I highly recommend that you read Harold's book. It will change your life if you take its principles to heart.
- *Irv Widmer, Author of The Gift Of Wealth*
www.IrvWidmer.com

"Harold's words and wisdom will allow you to become the leader you deserve to be!"
- *Jeffery Combs, Author of More Heart Than Talent*
www.GoldenMastermind.com

Acknowledgments

I would like to extend my special thanks to all of my immediate family and friends, the important people in my life who have assisted me in reaching my present destination.

Special thanks to my editor and adviser **Dr. Frank Shaker** for his wonderful support and guidance in writing this book.

Special thanks to **Chaneta Lewis** for all of her love, support and encouragement during our long and wonderful friendship. Chaneta you are a great person and dear friend with wonderful talent, and I am fortunate to have you as my friend.

Special thanks to **Evelyn Coulson** for her friendship and continued support both in business and in my personal life. Thanks Evelyn for your unconditional love and support.

Special thanks to **Horace U. Grant**, my longest and best friend. We will always have a special connection through the Spiritual Energy Field of All Possibilities. Horace you are a great friend and brother.

Special thanks to my good friend **David Jacobs** for his creative contribution to this project. The cover design and artwork for this book is awesome.

Finally yet most importantly, I would like to give my deepest gratitude to **René Dickerson** for her unconditional love, friendship, and support. Thanks René for believing in me during a period of my life when many people counted me out. René you are my Angel in every since of the word.

About the Author

Harold has one purpose in life: to inspire people to live to their highest potential. He has dedicated his life to teaching the success principles that allow people to recognize the true power that is within them. He firmly believes you can and will improve your life with the help of his philosophy. But you must make a choice: to apply the Universal Laws and Principles to your own life and business.

Harold teaches Personal Impact. In his view, personal impact is about your ability to see through all the illusions you encounter in life, to decide what you really want to experience in your life, and then to take the proper actions to manifest your dreams.

Central to Harold's work has been the theme that one has the infinite potential to grow, expand, and contribute to others no less than to oneself simply by applying the Universal Laws.

Harold is a writer and inspirational speaker, life/success coach, and successful entrepreneur. He has worked tirelessly in search of spiritual truth, one that makes a positive difference. He has banked his whole success on it.

His message? The Spirit can do for us only what it can do through us.

When Harold speaks about Life he does it with passion, because his vision is larger than he is—it's larger than any single individual. The philosophy he offers to people—both clients and readers of his teachings—is only the vehicle for greater things, not an end in itself.

This is the vision that inspires his teachings: Building a Prosperity Consciousness. Only the consciousness of prosperity will reverse the negative trend we see all around toward poor health and poverty. In this book, Harold shares a knowledge that will make a real difference in your life. In his words, "There is a better way. Just take a closer look at your real self. Ponder its potential, because it is infinite!"

Harold promotes mental patterns that satisfy life's deepest concerns. And he does it with urgency, because the benefits of these "patterns" are too compelling to pass.

Harold is dedicated to sharing prosperity with others. But prosperity is meaningless if it stands alone. There is no prosperity without health. Indeed, health is the Real Wealth. "Loose your health and you've lost everything," he insists.

Prosperity is equally meaningless without faith. Here, Harold speaks from the heart. Faith has sustained him throughout his life, helping transcend life's toughest challenges. He has helped many men and women accomplish their dreams, not by adapting to something out there in the world, but by assisting them in becoming the persons they already are. It takes faith to be able to do that, but then no faith is beyond anyone's reach.

Harold is living proof of this truth. However, personal success is not nearly enough if no one else can benefit from the knowledge he has gained after years of coaching individuals and his own personal development. He wishes prosperity on everyone, and he will do everything in his power to affirm positive thinking in place of the negative thinking that plagues our society.

He has the patience to help people turn their lives toward the affirmative—no matter what their measure of success may be—by optimizing their minds. And given his zeal, he's eminently qualified for the task. The gleam in his eyes is only a minute reflection of the effervescent life that animates his personality.

Read on and join him in this wondrous journey of discovery and you'll see what he means when he says, "It's not a question of how you will achieve your greatness, but when!"

Table of Contents

Foreword by Jeffery Combs   iii

Acknowledgments   vi

About the Author   vii

CHAPTER 1
Moving the Stars: An Introduction   1

CHAPTER 2
The Spiritual Energy Field of All Possibility   15

CHAPTER 3
You Are to Your Individual World What
Spirit Is to the Universe   35

CHAPTER 4
Your Words Work for You or Against You   49

CHAPTER 5
The Impact of Relative Filters on Your Words   77

CHAPTER 6
Discovering Your Star-Moving Power   89

CHAPTER 7
Using Your Star-Moving Power   109

CHAPTER 8
Speaking Your Words to Move Your Stars   131

Table of Contents

CHAPTER 9
Perfect Health Consciousness   143

CHAPTER 10
Prosperity Consciousness   169

CHAPTER 11
Empowering Relationships   191

CHAPTER 12
Moving the Stars in Your Life   207

CHAPTER 13
Creating Miracles with Your Words:
Four Case Studies and a Conclusion   217

Moving the Stars: An Introduction

– Harold Davis once said:
>   *If we had faith the size of a grain of sand, we could move the stars with our words.*

Imagine a night when the sky is clear and the stars are bright, you look up at the stars and at the top of your voice speak: **"Move, stars!"**

You patiently wait, but nothing happens.

Naturally, you wonder if there was something wrong with the way you said your words. So you regroup, this time with more determination and will power. **"Move, stars!"**

Still the stars do not move for you.

You might believe that it's impossible for you to move the stars with your words. I am here to tell you that it is possible.

What you are capable of doing as a spiritual being will astound you. As human beings, we grow used to settling for less, and less can be pretty disappointing.

It is now time that you be the Creative Factor in your life and start moving the stars with your words. You have a power that flows through you, around you, and from you. This power has no beginning and no end. It is everywhere present, all the knowledge and power there is. Because you are in this power and a part of it, you can move the stars with your words.

Moving the Stars With Your Words
By Harold Davis, Msc.D., Ph.D

Human beings are made of flesh and blood; their bodies can move because they're built of muscle, sinew, and heavy bone material. We pride ourselves for being more mobile than the sea cucumbers and urchins, but we are even better at moving things. We can move mountains, erect dams, divert great rivers. We sail ships laden with huge cargo, and fly millions of people across continents. No other animal on this planet rivals our capacity to move things through machines.

You will no doubt answer that we can do all this because of our intelligence. Intelligence is only part of the story. Other species inhabiting our world act in ways that exhibit some form of intelligence, so intelligence alone is not the only trait that renders us uniquely human.

Above all, we are spiritual beings. Being spiritual is vastly more important than having a calculating intelligence. As a spiritual being, you have a power that flows through you, around you, and from you. This power has neither beginning nor end; it is both knowledge and action.

Think about it for a moment, because spirituality is a power that encompasses each one of us. Every person is part of an all-encompassing Power that is infinitely greater than his or her individual will power and infinitely higher than the sum of the parts.

Spiritual Power (Creative Power) is what will enable you to reach out into the stellar zone and move any object, circumstance, or condition in your life in the way that you want to move it. Creative Power is the key to moving the stars in your personal life no matter what your stars may be. You might have a serious health challenge; maybe you have a great business ideal for solving a problem that affects the human race, or you may just want to live a joyous life filled with rich experiences. Whatever your stars are, you have the right and the power to move them, because you are a co-creator!

We Co-create Life

In the Universe, you are a co-creator, nothing less.

Physical or intellectual effort, by itself, will not produce the results that you expect or that best reflect what you think is the truth about you. You are with Spirit. Its power within you is manifested in every aspect of your mental and physical life, the same invisible power that has created you from the union of two cells and by which your heart continues to beat. It circulates your blood through arteries, capillaries, and veins. It gives you life and energy.

Spirit also gives you a special kind of consciousness.

Think of what a miracle human consciousness is. It is one thing to be here and now—so is the pebble in a fast-running mountain brook!—but entirely another to be a sentient being and aware that you are here. This is called self-consciousness. It is a gift of sight which allows you not only to perceive but also to think about the myriad color distinctions before you in this world—to admire or worry about them, to question or meditate on their importance.

Just look at yourself in the mirror. What color of eyes do you have? Is your hair blond, black, graying, or are you bald? Feel those muscles in your arms. Whatever your stature, whether you're a man or a woman, simple muscle tissue can combine into a pulling force that measures in tons. We all have heard the stories about the mother who lifts a car off her trapped child. It's true. Muscles do give us physical stamina and mobility—but that's only relative to other species.

Now look inside you.

You've got "spiritual muscles" here too, except that they are limitless. Every man and woman possesses them. We have strengths so extraordinary we can't get ourselves to believe they really exist and are so powerful. So we dismiss our inner muscles or, if we happen to sense them, ignore the power that moves them for fear of losing control of our lives.

There is a perfectly good reason why many people react in this way. During our waking hours, we all rely on our calculating minds to plan ahead and steer ourselves through careers that we may or may not like. But when we try to control our spiritual gifts in the same way we would the family car, the mind will prove a fickle friend indeed. As a result, most of us end up banishing the conscious use of Creative Power altogether from our lives for fear of losing control of life.

This is truly regrettable, because in doing so we impoverish our lives.

The Creative Factor

Our imagination comprises our spiritual muscles—our creativity. And no other gift gives us greater power than our creative faculty. I am not telling you to stop using your mental or physical muscles because I have this miracle formula that will bring you instant wealth or health by some form of magic. Like the muscles in your arms and legs, dreams have to be nurtured before you can get to your most cherished destination. Unfortunately, instead of nurturing them, we consign them along with our creative faculty to some obscure corner in our consciousness—because we have only short-term goals in our sights that we believe to be humanly possible to achieve.

Life does not have to be this way. We need not forget our dreams.

In writing this book, I want you to understand the power that flows through you, around you, and from you, because this is the very power that can move stars in your life. It will

Moving the Stars: An Introduction

transform you and make you the Creative Factor—both in your personal life and that of others.

Speak Your Words

The creative process I'm talking about empowers you to co-create your life by speaking your greatest dreams into existence. I call this speaking your words.

Speak your words and you will find that, whatever your failings or limitations, moving the stars becomes more than just a metaphor. It is a metaphor only with respect to the goals you leave unrealized. Once you begin to realize your dreams, you will see the reality behind this metaphor, a power so awesome and self-evident you'll wonder how you managed to ignore it for so long.

It doesn't matter whether you have a big or small dream, or that all you want is to leave a legacy for your children and grandchildren. You have the power to realize it. Once you see it in your mind's eye, it will be as real to you as the life and vitality that courses through your veins. Just imagine yourself rising out of the valley and up the mountain of life. On the mountain's peak you can see for miles around you and there is nothing blocking your view. You see life for what it really is. The valley of life, on the other hand, is crowded and you can only see what is in front of you.

What This Book Will Do For You

In Moving the Stars With Your Words, I will guide you through several steps that will help you reach the mountain peak of your life. Based on my insights into spiritual experience, I will show you how to find the Source of this

Moving the Stars With Your Words
By Harold Davis, Msc.D., Ph.D

experience—the source of all created things—and then to use the Universal Laws and Principles by which it unfolds to co-create what you, and only you, choose to experience in your life.

You're probably wondering what I mean by laws and principles and the source.

Universal Laws and Principles are the building blocks of your life and mine—indeed, of all life. By the time you finish reading this book, you will be consciously applying them to co-create a life that is worth living. In other words, you will learn to be the Creative Factor in your life. To be this Creative Factor, you must decide to recognize your own true potential. Once you've taken this momentous decision, you will learn to align yourself with the Source of everything created in the universe.

The alignment I'm referring to is extraordinarily powerful—beyond any single individual to comprehend. This is why going to the Source is so critical. It will enable you to co-create your life and experiences by the power of your words, thoughts, and feelings. The daily practice of this philosophy will empower you to manifest an abundance of the things you want most to have—health, wealth, and happiness—from the world of unrealized potential…and to move the stars.

Before we go through the various steps you need in order to move the stars in your life, let me first give you a bird's eye view of the main concepts used in this book.

THE MAIN CONCEPTS
The Energy Field

We live within the Spirit called the Spiritual Energy Field of All Possibilities. This may at first sound a little abstract, but at no time in our lives can we do without the full support of this spiritual energy field. This is true whether we are aware of it or not. Spiritual Energy flows through all created things; it is the awesome power that moves the stars.

If this view seems to go against the grain of conventional thinking, it does—if by "conventional" you mean fuzzy, superficial thinking that usually misses the reality behind things. The person who doggedly sticks to this way of seeing the world is content with appearances and the mediocrity of appearances.

It requires courage and focus to look and think in the way I'm suggesting. To help you along, I can give you the insight I have drawn from my own personal challenges, but in the end it makes no difference whose insight you learn from, as long as you learn to move your own stars, whatever they may be.

The star you want to move may be a health or career challenge, or some other goal of personal significance to you. You'll have every opportunity to put the insights I offer in this book to the test. However, please don't move on to the next section without first digesting this thought and making the commitment. What you will be able to accomplish—after you've put my insights to the test—will surprise you. You will have the power to move the stars in your life by speaking your words.

Moving the Stars With Your Words
By Harold Davis, Msc.D., Ph.D

Metaphysical Science and Principles

The philosophy of this book is based on Metaphysical Science and Principles. This science and these principles consist in the internal and external study of the nature of being and causality (that is, how things are causally related to each other). It is the study of Spirit, Mind, and Body—or, simply put, the study of life itself.

Applying these principles correctly will consciously release an inner power within you that remains under your control and nobody else's. Dispel every fear of losing that control, your inner power will set you free from every lack and limitation.

On a cosmic scale, you might think that such a task is insignificant, but that's not true at all. Every effort you undertake contributes something to the Universe. At a personal level, the freedom you experience in your consciousness will have a positive impact on many people around you. It will transform you into a major factor in their lives as their consciousnesses rises in causal relation to yours.

Three Powerful Realizations

This book will inspire you to co-create your life through three powerful realizations, which will act as your foundation:

> *The first realization is when you sense the presence of a higher power in the universe that I call Spirit.*
>
> *The next realization is when you know that this Spirit is all the power there is in the universe and that everything created comes from Spirit in its own basic form.*

Moving the Stars: An Introduction

The last realization is when you become a spiritual being who has learned to sense the presence of the higher power within yourself and in others.

The higher power is accessible everywhere. We use it all the time and in every part of our existence, whether we are conscious of it or not. This power works automatically and it will either manifest what you want in your life or, if you're not conscious of it, sometimes what you don't want. Your thoughts, words, and feelings determine the quality and quantity of its flow through you, because it works: first, by what I call the Law of Your Being; and second, by its willingness to express itself through you and into your mental and physical life. By becoming the things on which you consciously or unconsciously focus your words, thoughts, and feelings.

The Wrong Power

We have all been fooled, at one time or another, into believing we are creative because we act in a certain way. Most of the time, we have been using our will power with nothing to show for its use but the personal energy expended. The trouble is that it takes real power to co-create our life. Trying to co-create life through sheer will power can be exhausting, which accounts for why so many folks feel that life's hardships are so insurmountable.

The question you ought to be asking is this: How can I make my life easier?

You can start by thinking of will power only as a means. Will power is vastly more efficient as a mental tool to focus real power, as opposed to power for its own sake. Whatever you imagine this power to be, it ought to be working in your

Moving the Stars With Your Words
By Harold Davis, Msc.D., Ph.D

favor. More than that and it will burn you out. Use it, first, to align yourself with real power, and second, to build an image in your mind's eye of what you want.

This will work much better.

Real or creative power works by the Law of Corresponding. By that I mean corresponding with Spirit. It's another way of saying that Spirit accepts your words, thoughts, and feelings; that it takes them and, through real power, faultlessly converts them into a real life event in your physical world.

I know this must sound awfully vague right now — or worse, magical — but bear with me a while longer. The concept Law of Corresponding is based on the same Universal Law that takes the genetic information contained in a seed and uses it to manifest a plant from the soil in which that seed has been sown. The amazing thing is not that the Universal Law does this, but that it should do it so precisely that it humbles our best biologists, despite their wealth of knowledge in genetics.

The same principle is at work spiritually. Let me show you how.

Every event in your life sprouts from a potential state through the information contained in — let me call it — a "thought spore." Same principle. The process has to be just as precise as that of a germinating carrot seed, or we'd be talking about something other than reality. Your thoughts cannot produce anything but what the combination of words and feelings consciously or unconsciously expressed by you dictate, any more than a carrot seed can produce a watermelon.

The Power of Choice

Spirit is the power that grants every individual his or her self-consciousness. Unlike human beings, dogs are not aware that they are dogs, nor can any animal know itself the way a human being does. Geese must fly south for the winter. Can you imagine a flock of geese deciding they want to travel east instead of south or north, because they just aren't up to it this year? That would be contrary to their nature, right?

Self-consciousness involves far more than just being conscious of your presence or your body, or recognizing other members of your species for the purpose of mating or hunting in packs. Which brings to mind a fable I once heard about a scorpion and a bird.

A bird perched at the edge of a cliff was about to fly across to the other side of the valley when a scorpion came along and interrupted him. The scorpion politely said, "Hmm, Mr. Bird, forgive my intrusion but I'd be mighty grateful if you'd fly me across this valley on your back."

The bird replied, "I may have a bird's brain but I'm not crazy. I know very well that, given the chance, a scorpion would sting a bird even my size."

"You're absolutely right about that, Mr. Bird, but you're not thinking clearly."

"How's that?"

"You see, sir, even if I wanted to, why, stinging you in midair would only plunge us both to our deaths."

The scorpion's explanation sounded reasonable enough, so the bird told him to crawl up on his back. No sooner had the bird and scorpion reached halfway across the valley than, sure enough, the scorpion stung him on his beautiful crest.

The bird couldn't believe it. As he and the scorpion were about to crash into the valley, he twisted his neck backward and asked the scorpion with a perplexed expression on his

Moving the Stars With Your Words
By Harold Davis, Msc.D., Ph.D

face, "Why did you sting me? I'm about to die and so are you!"

The scorpion replied in an even more perplexed tone, "What else could I do? It's my nature."

There is no chance that a bird and a scorpion would ever cooperate in the same way that two people with the power of choice could. It's against their natures, and animals — we all know — cannot act against their natures. But wait. Let's look at this a little more creatively and take it one step further.

People, unlike animals, are capable of acting against their inborn nature. In fact, we can behave contrary to our nature simply by saying: "I am such-and-such." This is possible because we have freedom of choice. Otherwise, what's the sense of "choosing" if our nature didn't allow it?

You, as a person, have the power to define yourself in any way you choose simply by filling in the blank that comes after "I am". All that your conscious mind has to do after that is start a new creative process based on your affirmation or denial. Everything else being equal, this process should bring you closer to any end you desire.

Now, take this a step higher.

Society is a collectivity, composed of many individual expressions in mind. But collectivity does not mean chaos. The awesome power of the Spiritual Energy Field of All Possibilities (Spirit & Law) connects us together through a single mind that permits us to recognize each other, communicate, and share our experiences. It is through this connection that a single collective thought process takes place called the Collective Consciousness.

If each one of us ran against his or her nature, think of the consequences that would surely follow. There would be no collective thought process left to talk about, let alone a single inspiring thought or the reality it needs to manifest itself.

Try it out on your own. Record what your negative thoughts manifest in the physical world. Human beings are obsessed with what doesn't work in the physical universe, rather than what works, so that shouldn't be a problem. I can guarantee you it will be neither inspiring nor spiritual.

Embrace the Truth

Whether the manifestations of your thoughts are inspiring or uninspiring, positive or negative, embrace the truth fully as you find it and go from there.

Doing so will earn you a starring role in your life that is worthy of your place as the Creative Factor. Lying to yourself will gain you little. It won't empower you to create your life exactly the way you want it to be, because your words—true or false—are a Law unto your life.

When you are truthful, you are in perfect harmony with the living Spirit that flows through you, around you, and from you. Alignment with your Source will free you. You will see the world as it really is and begin to move the stars in your life using your words.

Notes

The Spiritual Energy Field of All Possibilities

– Horace Grant and Harold Davis once said:
Nothing comes to a sleeper but a dream... It's time to wake up!

By now, I hope you are at least aware that there might be a power in the universe that responds to your words, thoughts, and feelings. This power has created the heavens and the earth; it causes the stars to move, planets to rotate, and seeds to grow. It has created us in its likeness. It imparts its values to us. It takes us into its embrace and makes us part of it. This is the power I call the Spiritual Energy Field of All Possibilities.

Spirit is the Spiritual Energy Field of All Possibilities

The Spiritual Energy Field of All Possibilities (Spirit & Law) is everything. It is all the knowledge and power that exists, but it has neither beginning nor end. There is no space or time in which this energy field does not reach. As a field of energy, it is the absolute cause of our existence.

It is also what Spirit encompasses. You might know Spirit by some other name—God, if you're a religious person, or infinite intelligence, if you're scientifically inclined. For our purpose, what you call it is less important than how you define its energy field. In other words, it is all the power there is, all the knowledge there is, and it is everywhere present.

Here is my definition:

> *Spirit, or the Spiritual Energy Field of All the Possibilities it encompasses, is omnipotent, omniscient, and omnipresent.*

This precise definition encompasses every aspect of the Spiritual Energy Field of All Possibilities (Spirit & Law), and is the key to understanding the ideas presented in this book. If you want to benefit fully from these ideas, you need to adopt it.

Remember, the spiritual energy field I am referring to stands for ever-changing life. It affects everything that resides in it and everything, literally, is in it. It is the power that flows through you, around you, and from you. Spiritual energy (creative energy) can cause your body's energy supply to fall or rise. Therefore, a negative worldview will bring about a negative energy flow in the body; a positive worldview will bring about a positive one.

Despite this, it is easy to forget that negative and positive energies are both spiritual. They create a thought atmosphere that vibrates at a certain frequency determined only by the words, thoughts, and feelings that make up our worldview (or vision). When your worldview is life giving, you attract conditions, people, and circumstances that vibrate at that particular frequency. When your worldview is life depleting, you attract conditions, people, and circumstances in harmony with that. It's very important that you use this creative energy in a way that works for you, not against you. When your thoughts cause the creative energy to create a negative energy flow in your body, the "inner muscles" grow weaker. When they cause a positive flow of creative energy, the muscles grow stronger.

I cannot overemphasize how important this point is. It offers a way to interface with the Spiritual Energy Field of All Possibilities (Spirit and Law), which you can use to answer purposeful questions about life and to create a thought atmosphere that attracts healthy conditions and experiences.

Something akin to this happens when a farmer plants his seeds. Each seed contains the blueprint for a specific plant; the soil then receives this information and provides the seed with the substances it needs to become this plant. The Spiritual Energy Field is no different. It is about the same power and it fructifies in the same way.

This, in short, is why I call the source of creative energy the Spiritual Energy Field of All Possibilities and define Spirit in the manner that I did.

Discovering the Thought Atmosphere

A few paragraphs above, I introduced a concept which may not yet be familiar to you—thought atmosphere. Let me illustrate what I mean by this concept.

A few years ago, while I was working out at a California high school track, I happened to cut across an open field after finishing my daily track workout, when I noticed a man training his dog. They were about two hundred feet away. After pausing for a few seconds to size me up, the dog started running toward me at full clip. The dog's trainer began shouting commands in an attempt to get him to stop, but to no avail. His dog was unstoppable.

Two things immediately struck me about my situation: the dog was very big and it was up to no good. Once I grasped this, a peace came over me that compelled me to stop in my tracks. I decided to wait for my attacker.

Curiously, when it got to where I was standing, the dog ran up against me as if trying to slow itself down. It had expected me to run, and when I refused to budge, it circled and brushed up against me a second time, this time snapping and baring its teeth, as though daring me to fight back. By then, the owner arrived—completely out of breath, having run nonstop across the field. He quickly separated the dog from me and put it back on its leash.

The dog appeared to be confused at this unexpected outcome. Its instincts told it that a piece of me, a bipedal prey, should have made a nice snack; or it was just being territorial, with the intention of sinking its teeth into my flesh for the sheer pleasure of it. Whatever its plan, I refused to cooperate. And it was easier than I thought. Quick analysis of the circumstances allowed me to change the most likely outcome had fear overtaken me, and I decided to make a run for it.

In other words, my consciousness produced a thought atmosphere that did not support the dog's intent, because it was a consciousness of peace, not one of fear or aggression.

My purpose for sharing this story with you is not to boast about how brave I am in the face of danger, but to illustrate how higher consciousness will prevail every time and in any similar situation. It's the Law of Consciousness.

How We Relate to Spirit

How each of us relates to Spirit is the most vital aspect of our lives. There are mainly four ways in which we do it:

The first way is based on a relationship of separation from Spirit. This relationship may be broken down into several kinds of experiences.

The Spiritual Energy Field of All Possibilities

We may:

- *Seek a relationship with Spirit.*
- *Shun our relationship with Spirit.*
- *Believe we have no need for a relationship with Spirit.*
- *Believe we are unworthy of a relationship with Spirit.*

Each of these experiences implies some kind of separation from Spirit—including the first, which assumes an initial separation.

The second way of relating to Spirit is through an awareness of this Spirit. This awareness might have emerged after a striking personal experience that showed us the possibilities of a relationship with Spirit. Or, we may know of someone who had very rapidly transformed his or her financial life through acquired wealth. You may know another person who recovered from a disease that had been diagnosed as incurable. Awareness alone could inspire a willingness to learn more about Spirit—for example, through books, religious services, or seminars.

The third way is when we seek to recapture a feeling we had during a star-moving experience. We may choose to do this through daily meditations with a view to achieving an ongoing connection with Spirit.

The fourth way, which holds the greatest promise, represents our true relationship with Spirit. Here we are one with Spirit, and yet Spirit continues to be greater than we are. It flows through us, around us, and from us. It is all the power there is, all the knowledge there is, and it is everywhere present. Everything is within the grasp of its power and we are an important part of its power. Thanks to this we are able to move the stars in our life.

Moving the Stars With Your Words
Harold Davis, Msc.D., Ph.D

Review Your Life

I invite you to think back a little and remember at least one star-moving experience you've benefited from. Almost everyone has had one such life experience. Any event that triggered star-moving feelings inside you would qualify. Some of us are enamored of certain technological advances, especially those that affect our lives in some particular way; others are impressed by unusual or harrowing experiences in their own lives. Maybe something happened in your life that precipitated a salutary change inside you, but not before, causing you to be fearful.

Perish the fear! If you believe that the event has changed you for the better, there is no reason on earth why you should fear it. Spirit protects as it transforms.

These snippets from the past are more significant than we'd like to admit, because they make us aware of how the power manifests itself in our lives.

Try it.

When I first began to reflect seriously on my past experiences, it didn't take me long to discover one star-moving experience after another. I don't think that makes me more important than the next person. All I know is that those events have brought me closer to the most important presence in my life—Spirit. Let me give you a good example, a life-threatening situation from which I barely escaped with my life.

In 1977, I accepted a position at a Texas gas plant, where all new technical employees were required to participate in a company-sponsored orientation program. The program was designed to assess how much a new plant employee was committed to the company and the job before permanent status was granted. It had to do it through tedious work assignments unrelated to the job, the idea being to weed out

The Spiritual Energy Field of All Possibilities

anyone too uncommitted to accept these assignments and to offer a right of passage to those loyal enough not to refuse.

One morning, my supervisor asked me to mow the grass in a remote part of the gas plant property where there was a levy. A levy is nothing more than a big ditch with water flowing through it and grass growing on both sides. The sides in this one were sloped at approximately 20- to 30-degree angles. An old yellow tractor was placed at my disposal that had a front-end loader installed on it. This feature gave its operation additional complexity which nothing in my experience had prepared me for. Until then, I had been living in the city and had never before driven a tractor, let alone one with a loader.

In no time, I found myself sliding down the levy, having failed to lower the front-end loader. I had no idea it was too elevated for safe operation on a sloped surface. So I shifted the weight of the tractor, but that only compounded my predicament. Once the law of gravity began working against me and the tractor started sliding down toward the water in the levy, it was apparent that no positive outcome was possible.

The trouble was that I couldn't just jump off the tractor to my left—the slope was too steep. Nor could I jump off to the front or the back; the front-end loader and the mower blades were in the way. There was no place for me to jump at all. The future looked utterly bleak for me.

I have a vivid recollection of this event up to this point, because everything seemed to happen in slow motion. Instinctively, I had given myself up to Spirit's care. It was the only thing left for me to do. This mental action must have triggered something inside me, because suddenly all stood still and I saw myself going into the water—ahead of the tractor. The amazing thing was that the water into which I fell did not restrict me or retard my movements in any way. The next thing I saw was the tractor flipped upside down in the water, its wheels in the air and the motor still running.

When I came to my senses, I realized that I was on the opposite side of the levy: at the top viewing the event from afar. I knew that it had taken no more than a few seconds for all this to happen, but in my mind's eye it was much, much longer.

One puzzling question immediately entered my mind:

How did I avoid sinking down into the water and thereby escape bodily harm?

As often as I have pondered this question, to this day I have found no satisfactory answer. It's not as if nine ways to escape serious injury or death lay before me for my choosing. I was in dire straights. In the thick of it, however, I hardly thought about the terrible outcome that awaited me. I simply let Spirit completely take over the situation.

This may not be much of an explanation, but what other viable rationale could possibly account for the strange outcome? I was plucked from the jaws of death when everything around me said I was trapped and about to die.

Spirit had solved the unsolvable.

I'm telling you this story not as personal testimony for the truth of magic but because the consequences of my actions were strange but true. These actions emanated from a different center in my mind, such that Spirit rescued my body through me. As soon as I let go of the life-and-death mire in which I was hopelessly caught, faith seeped through me and protected me from physical harm in a way I cannot reasonably describe without reference to Spirit as the principal cause of my rescue.

Cause and effect happened in precisely that order.

This was the star-moving event that saved my life and taught me about the real power at work. I'm grateful it happened to me, because at least now I can share the story with you. It's kind of like returning from the dead, I know, except it is more believable. I'll tell you why.

You may choose to deny the assumption that a person pronounced medically dead was really dead before returning to life. In my case, there is no assumption either to deny or to accept. I come to you after an observable fact.

My rescue simply happened. It taught me the importance of letting go of certain situations to a higher power. Spirit worked through me to move my stars, and it will work through you.

Sometimes We Fail

The power that flows through you, around you, and from you can lift your life to the highest level. It can heal you; create perfect health, and happiness. It can cause peace and understanding and eliminate discord in your life. This power will move the stars for you. But you must choose to use it in your life.

Sometimes we fail. This is an unavoidable fact of life. But if Spirit works through us, you may ask, why do we sometimes fail to produce the results we aim for?

Whatever the awesome creativity of Spirit, we stumble over things great and small. Life throws up all kinds of challenges. The irony is that we can sometimes overcome huge challenges more easily than those that seem small or trivial. Whatever the size of the challenge, there are reasons for your failure, but they are all reducible to a single root.

We fail because our subconscious mind is cluttered with thoughts that are contrary to what we really want, and who we really are.

Everyone suffers from this, even the best among us. It is only human. But that doesn't mean we must resign ourselves to it.

The presence of contrary thoughts in your mind spawns a condition that impels you to blame something outside of yourself for what your own mind was bound to produce by law.

Look at it this way. Your years of childhood were influenced by your parents, environment, peers, and all the events that together form the bulk of your waking experience. You are also influenced by what society determines to be life's incontrovertible truths—the realities that most people accept without question.

The result is a person who is mystified as to why he has failed in this or that respect, despite all the effort he has put in. Everything should have added up. There seems to be no rational explanation why it hasn't.

We all experience this at one time or another, forgetting that Spirit does for us only what it can do through us. This is the key.

Therefore, here is the question you should ask yourself: What is the level of my consciousness? Because the contrariness inside your mind keeps resisting Spirit. That's the real obstacle to your success.

Mind in Action

Everything is created in the mind first. What you experience in life happens as a result of your mind in action. And the mind has two aspects that are responsible for personal experiences. There is the conscious mind and there is the subconscious mind.

I will fully cover these two aspects of mind a little later in this chapter. What you want to understand from this discussion is that your conscious mind is the builder of the subconscious mind, but also that your subconscious mind creates your life.

The interaction of these two aspects of mind is what is called the Law of Mind in Action.

What Determines Our Choice

For a number of years, I have been searching for an answer to the question: What empowers a person to make the right choices in life? After a while, I began to realize that the answer made sense only to the person who desires to be the Creative Factor in his or her life. Choice ought to put you before a truth that sets you free.

The right choices can only come through you. They must emerge from a pure source of knowledge that exists in the Spiritual Energy Field of All Possibilities (Spirit & Law). This is not to say that you cannot select by observing the conditions in your life and using this information as a basis for decision-making at a certain level. Nothing says you should not do it, but relying on this approach alone will not bring about true success.

If you want to be confident that your choice comes from the best possible source, you have to choose from the energy field that is first cause and omniscient.

Creating Destiny by Choice

When I was a young boy growing up in Houston, TX, I made a conscious choice not to be a part of the problems that my material deprivation had created in my life. It was one of my earliest star-moving experiences and it did not depend on the visible options that lay before me at the time.

Thankfully, I also had friends. We knew the streets of Houston pretty well, and I felt tremendous pressure to conform to their way of thinking. There were many other influences coming from family and, later, colleagues and associates. Seeing all these people daily created a social environment that made for plenty of temptation to choose the unproductive things in my life. Various opportunities presented themselves to me, no doubt, yet the odds were not in my favor to turn my life around and to choose the affirmative. Despite these odds, I made a conscious choice to co-create something different. In hindsight, I know that I succeeded in co-creating freedom from them. But I had to make a choice, first and foremost, not merely a selection.

You make a real choice by imagining the possibility of choosing something different, as opposed to simply excepting what lies in front of you or whatever happens to be manifested as a result of someone else's choices.

There is no way around making conscious choices if you want to be able to move the stars with your words. You must have the conviction to do what you want and nurture faith in a power that is greater than any of us.

Although I stayed the course on this magnificent journey, it took me a while to realize the true power of choice. Understanding how the Spiritual Energy Field of All Possibilities (Spirit and Law) works doesn't happen overnight.

Universal Laws Work for Us or Against Us

The Universal Laws that work through us do so either for or against us. There is plenty of scientific proof to back up this statement. Modern psychologists repeatedly point to the destructive effects that negative thoughts have on our personality, beliefs, and character. Such thoughts produce frustrations which studies in psychosomatic medicine have shown to be the principal cause of illnesses. These illnesses can be in our mind, our body, or our connections with the world.

No one can escape this reality.

Our lives are governed by Universal Laws and Principles that are older than time; as a matter of fact, they transcend time. They were not invented by people to justify their actions. We do not create Universal Laws but discover them in the course of living. Creating a Universal Law would be like manufacturing an antique chair. Buying such an "antique" would be a wasted investment, because there's nothing authentic or real about it.

When we discover Laws, you sometimes infer that luck plays a significant role in the process that leads to discovery. However, the Universe doesn't play favorites. Life is not about people being lucky in any situation. It is governed only by the same Laws and Principles for all. The master keys to success in any endeavor lies in your words, because your words operate by the Law of Cause and Effect and the Law of Mind in Action.

Earlier we spoke of failure as being an inescapable part of the human enterprise. Let us now put it in the right perspective in relation to the Laws. Failure indicates simply that you have followed the Law of Failure. Alternatively, success shows that you have followed the Law of Success.

You may try to deny this all you want, but there is no way to escape the effects of Universal Laws. Eventually, you will

Moving the Stars With Your Words
Harold Davis, Msc.D., Ph.D

have to face the truth, because truth alone will free you from failure. For every effect there is a corresponding cause. We cannot plant carrot seeds in the soil and hope that the carrot seed will produce watermelons. The Universe will not, and cannot, violate its own laws.

Think of thoughts as seeds. It is impossible to achieve success while being conscious only of failure. These are two paths that bear two different fruits. The Universe will give you success only when you learn to build a consciousness that translates into success.

Success is manifested by a spiritual method that unfolds so long as you maintain your consciousness of success. The idea is to realize that you have the ability to attain what you want to experience by choosing your thoughts. The conditions of your health and affairs will correspond exactly to your subconscious thoughts.

The good news in this is that dominion over your thoughts entails dominion over the conditions of your life!

The way to exercise this dominion is to choose the source of your knowledge, much like the information contained in a seed. You may choose an internal source, which is a pure source of knowledge; or you may choose a secondary source of information, which comprises your external conditions.

The Spiritual Energy Field of All Possibilities (Spirit and Law) is the power that gives you awareness of yourself and the power that animates your body. Once you believe that consciousness is energy, and that it is as real as gravity or electricity, it is a short distance from believing that you will be able to move the star with your words.

Many people ask me if speaking words is different from saying a prayer. My answer is: prayer is a request for some good to be given to me.

When you speak your words, you draw your good to yourself or to others through the operation of the Law of Attraction and the Law of Vibration.

Keep in mind, though, that results are the name of the game. When we speak our words we create a vibration inside of us that generates an inner emotion, which in turn causes something to happen beneath the surface of awareness deep inside our subconscious.

Words can create a vibration that attracts people, things, and circumstances vibrating at the same frequency that you are. This vibration is entirely dependent on the words, conviction, and faith which inhabit you in everything you do.

The Law must be applied with a definite purpose to cause new power to flow through all of your mind, body, and affairs.

Taking Responsibility

You must take responsibility for what has happened to you and what you have attracted in your life up to this point. Doing so will immediately cause a positive change in your life. Adopting a positive consciousness based on your conscious choice will enable the real power—which is what Spirit is—to flow through you. This will start the healing process in your mind, body, and in all of your affairs.

Two Activities of One Mind

In order to understand how mind creates things from your words, thoughts, and feelings, you must know that the mind exhibits two activities: "the conscious mind in action" and "the subconscious mind in action." These activities account for all the major functions of mind. They allow us to understand the way mind works. However, it is very important to remember that there is only one mind, which performs two different types of activities.

To grasp what I mean by two activities performed by a single mind, just think of an iceberg. The conscious mind is the tip, the subconscious mind the submerged part. This distinction does not change the fact that an iceberg is a single mass.

Failure to recognize the two types of activities of the mind causes confusion, unhappiness, sickness, and poverty in our lives. Understanding their differences and how to apply this understanding will manifest health and prosperity. By learning the differences, you can more easily abandon activities that fail to support your dreams, and choose those that do. It will allow you to create what you desire most in your life.

The Creative Mind

When you look at an iceberg above the surface of the ocean, what do you see? Only a small part of the whole mass, right? That is the information of which you become aware by way of your conscious mind. It happens with ordinary perception. However, there is more to the iceberg than meets the eye and it lies below the surface. The information beneath your conscious awareness is located in your subconscious mind.

The main point to remember from this analogy is that what lies below the surface exerts the most powerful influence. It gives the iceberg the power to damage a great "unsinkable" ship like the Titanic. The size and depth of the submerged portion of the iceberg is where all potential power lies. Likewise, the subconscious mind contains most of the knowledge—in fact, an infinite amount of knowledge. Being below the surface of our awareness, it has a powerful impact on our lives.

I can't overemphasize the importance of this aspect of our mind. You must not only be aware of it but also understand its functions.

The Subconscious Mind Must Accept

The conscious and the subconscious work together in your mind. The subconscious must accept the words, thoughts, and feelings which the conscious gives it. Then it must turn these into experiences, such as a job, home, car, money, or whatever else you want in your life. This is what most distinguishes the conscious from the subconscious mind.

Beneath the surface of your awareness, the subconscious mind works constantly to turn good and bad thought-seeds into the manifested conditions of your life. But it has no power to choose. You mustn't lose sight of this. The subconscious never reasons with or refuses to take what the conscious mind gives to it. It must always work from a pattern. It has no choice in the matter. The pattern of thought it needs comes from the conscious mind. And just as the soil accepts any seed, so the subconscious part of your mind accepts any thought-seed it receives.

A farmer decides what type of crop he wants to have come harvest time. He may plant a row of tomatoes, another of carrots, and a third of corn. The soil accepts all his seeds and provides a harvest based on his choice of seeds.

The thoughts you harbor in your mind are the thoughts that will manifest themselves for you, whether by conscious choice or through the part of your mind that lies below the conscious level. This choice is passed into the subconscious mind just like a seed that is planted into the soil. Your thought-seeds will then begin to grow in your mental soil. They will continue to work and act automatically until they are replaced or uprooted by your conscious mind.

This, in sum, is the process by which we co-create everything that we experience in life.

Mind Creates From a Pattern

Your habitual thought-patterns are located at some level of consciousness. They are nothing more than your personal history and choices repeating themselves according to the Law of Mind in Action.

A negative attitude results when the negative thoughts submerged in your subconscious mind are repeated and crystallize into a habit. A happy attitude can become a habit when you consciously choose positive thoughts. It is not by special gift that some people are blessed with a positive personality and others are afflicted with negative personalities. Each of us has the ability to choose the attitude we desire. Subconscious mind gives form to our choices.

You can raise the level of your subconscious thought-pattern by using your conscious mind. This is a process that produces the outer circumstances of your life, because it creates your self-image. Subconscious mind is omniscient (all-knowing), and by definition has access to infinite resources of knowledge. However, personal memory is your personal connection to the subconscious mind. The subconscious mind knows how to create any condition effortlessly, and it does this without caring what it creates.

Everything manifested in our Universe is a product of the subconscious mind. All creation happens in the mind of Spirit, and since everything is in the mind of Spirit, our conscious mind and our personal memory are in that one mind.

Stray Thoughts

Some thoughts enter into our subconscious mind below conscious awareness. The reason is that it is impossible for us to be conscious of everything happening in our lives all at once. There are many stray thoughts that find their way into our mental garden, much as the weed-seeds are blown by the wind into a planted garden and mix with the good seeds.

It is important that you clear your mind of thought-seeds you don't want. This will allow your dominant thought-seeds, or thought patterns, to stay pure. They will allow your subconscious mind to manifest what you really desire in life — and to move the stars for you!

Speaking Your Words
to Clear Your Consciousness

Let me give you an excellent example of how you can clear your consciousness of unwanted thoughts by speaking your words, and thereby align yourself with the flow of the Spiritual Energy Field of All Possibilities (Spirit and Law). Here is how a person who acts decisively to this end would think:

> *I realize that I am a spirit in The Spirit. That Spirit is perfect and complete, and I am one with this perfect power.*
>
> *Peace, joy, and happiness surround me and flow through everything I think, say, and do.*
>
> *There is a deep calmness at the center of my being, a perfect understanding of my relationship with Spirit.*

My thoughts rest in peace and joy and in cheerful expectation of my good.

As I become conscious of the unconditional love of my Creator, I shed all lack, all fear all that is false from my experience of life.

My expectation of life guides me into complete joy and happiness. The way is made clear before me. All is well in my consciousness, so all is well in my life.

And so it is.

You Are to Your Life What Spirit Is to the Universe

– Harold Davis once said:
> A drop of water is not the ocean, but it is of the same quality as the ocean.

Spirit created the Universe. It is the First Cause. You now know that all things are created from its spiritual energy field and that this Spiritual Energy Field of All Possibilities (Spirit and Law) contains everything that exists. You also know that each person is an individualized part of this spiritual energy field who can share in its values. However, an individual is not just a part of the whole. The individual is to his or her life what Spirit is to the Universe.

In this chapter, you will discover how Spirit equally bestows the gift of life to everyone. It is by virtue of this gifting that all possibilities exist for us. I am not referring to just any power conjured up by my imagination. Spirit is all power!

We may be incapable of fully comprehending or representing it, but we can still get a glimpse of the process by which it creates the Universe.

Spirit, the Universal I Am

Spirit is the Universal I am because it is absolute in its presence and expression.

What does this mean?

Above all, it means that we must never refer to linear time or to space as we think about Spirit's activities. Spirit is omnipresent, whereas we are not. We are finite in our present and infinite only in our ability to think through Spirit.

You need to understand this, but how you do it is just as important. The omnipotence of Spirit and how it works are evident only through faith.

The Invisible Cause

Spirit is the invisible cause of all things seen and unseen. Before we can study it and discover the Universal Laws through which it operates, we must observe the seen (manifested) Universe. Everything manifested obeys the Universal Laws. Spirit's Words comprise the eternal part where these Universal Laws operate. In short, they are the Laws of the Universe.

Spirit's words not only create everything, they do it by way of an evolving, mathematically expressible process that is responsible for the things we see and don't see in our physical world. We discover part of this creative process when we discover Universal Laws and how they operate at every level of the creative process.

We Live in a Spiritual Universe

We live in a spiritual universe that operates completely by Universal Laws. But Spirit, being omniscient, is also an infinite thinker. Its words are perfectly expressed on three manifested levels of expression: Spirit, Mind, and Body.

These levels are the process by which Spirit expresses the things inside it in a way that makes them exist. It is the process of the invisible becoming visible. The Universe is always evolving into a greater existence. This implies change, which is a natural process we refer to as the Law of Transmutation. It is absolutely futile to try to keep things from changing.

The Universe Is Perfect

The Universal Laws are completely independent of our role in the Universe. They are the Fundamental Principles of Life, which impacts on everything we see and do not see. These Laws are responsible for the process by which everything is created and manifested into the mental and physical Universe. However, Spirit is conscious of everything that exists, because it has made every existing thing out of itself, and by so doing becomes the thing it makes.

Albert Einstein described part of this Law of Transmutation in his famous equation $E=MC^2$. His equation explains that energy and mass are, mathematically, one and the same. His discovery has enabled mankind to develop a technology—for example, nuclear energy and the atomic bomb—that has not only changed the world but has proved the unity of all things. The discoveries that have resulted from Einstein's equation show that the Universe is a unity that is continually being created from one spiritual substance.

Everything is made from this substance; everything is made from creative energy that comes from the Spiritual Energy Field of All Possibilities (Spirit and Law).

The Universe is a Cosmos

The Universe is both perfect and cosmic in nature. Being a cosmos, it is in perfect harmony with itself. If it were not, it would be destroyed, since by definition the Spirit that animates it is omnipotent. It is inconceivable how all power in the universe could ever exist against all power. Wholeness and harmony are the natural state of the spiritual Universe.

What Can We Know About Spirit?

No one has ever seen Spirit. We can know something about its nature only by observing what it has manifested. We know from our earlier discussions that it may be broadly defined as omnipresent, omniscient, and omnipotent, and of course, that it is the Spiritual Energy Field of All Possibilities.

Scientists are presumably the most qualified people in our society to tell us about the Spiritual Energy Field of All Possibilities, because they are trained to extract hidden secrets from manifested results. They witness the power of the atom and subatomic particles though powerful microscopes and other instruments. They study the building blocks of life. They use giant telescopes to study the planets, stars, and the vastness of the Universe in general. They study the workings of the human body, with its miraculous abilities to maintain itself and to produce the Godlike effects we witness in our daily lives.

This is precisely what inspired Einstein to declare his wish to know the thoughts of God: everything else is just the details.

Yet Spirit also has values. You don't have to be a scientist to recognize its Values. Some of the Values of Spirit are observable simply by using the five senses and our feelings: **Unconditional Love, Order, Creativity, Wisdom, Perfection, Abundance, Harmony, Power, and Joy.**

Spirit Value UNCONDITIONAL LOVE.
Unconditional Love is more than just an emotion. It is a powerful energy that inspires and is inherently eternal, because it is what Spirit gives each of us. We live within the Energy Field of All Possibilities of Spirit, and by virtue of this have already received all the possible gifts.

These gifts are available to all alike. It doesn't matter if you're a saint or a sinner, black or white, rich or poor. In this specific sense, the sun shines on the just and the unjust alike. This truly is an example of the unconditional love of Spirit.

Spirit Value ORDER.
By studying the patterns of the Universe, we can observe the Order of Spirit and realize that we live in a universe governed by Universal Laws and Principles. This is much easier to do than we imagine.

We encounter the Law of Order every time we plant a carrot seed. After about eighty days, a carrot grows from this seed. Observe how our planet rotates on its axis. By doing so, it completes its pattern in exact time, with no variation.

We know that we can count on the Universal Laws to endure. If the patterns of these laws were to change, the result would be chaos and confusion. This is why the Universe is called a Cosmos rather than a Chaos.

Spirit Value CREATIVITY.
The creativity of Spirit is also clearly observable. We need only turn to the results of absolute power, which are all around us. We witness them in the unlimited varieties of species we see manifested in the plant and animal kingdoms; in the complexity and unique talents of human beings, etc. The applications of the Laws of the Universe are truly infinite. The creativity of Spirit is in plain view of everyone.

Spirit Value WISDOM. Spirit is Wisdom.
We see it in the healing of a flesh wound or the solving of a problem. It is the same Wisdom that guides the rose bush to seek the sunshine above and then struggle to extract what it needs from the soil in order to grow.

Spirit Value PERFECTION.
We attribute perfection to anything that is pure and lacking in no details. Spirit is perfect because it is omnipresent, omniscient, and omnipotent. The Universe would have destroyed itself a long time ago if it were not perfect and whole. It has everything within itself, and all can be traced back to one essential substance: Spiritual Energy. It has everything within itself.

Spirit Value ABUNDANCE.
Spirit is abundant in its nature, and we thrive in its abundance through the Universe we live in. To observe this abundance, all you need to do is look at any aspect of your life. Go to the ocean and watch the awesome power of the waves. Imagine what power drives these waves on to shore. You have no doubt wondered, at one time or another, how many grains of sand could possibly lie on a beach, or how many blades of grass grow in a farmer's field, or the drops of water that make up a lake.

If you are still unconvinced, then turn your eyes to the sky on a clear night. How many stars do you see? They are unlimited, all hanging in a space so vast we cannot begin to measure it.

Spirit Value HARMONY.
We can observe the harmony of Spirit thanks to the Law of Cause and Effect. It allows us to know that a good thought

produces good results and bad thoughts produce bad results. It also allows us to know that some things don't mix together.

Omnipotence, a major characteristic of Spirit, is all Power. But remember that all power excludes all other power. There can be no other where the power is all. Therefore, there is no other power that might oppose that of Spirit. If it were possible to have an opposing power, then universal power would destroy itself. All power against all power equals total destruction.

Spirit Value POWER.
The Power of Spirit is self-evident and needs no justification. It is plainly obvious that a tremendous Power operates effortlessly to keep all the planets, stars, and galaxies in the Universe on their courses. This power operates throughout the Universe without losing a single ounce of energy.

Spirit Value JOY. Spirit is Joy.
We observe this joy when we are in alignment with the Universe. The more joy we experience in life, the closer we are aligned with Spirit.

But Spirit can never be separated from itself, and we are always within Spirit. When we're not in a state of Joy we are separated from our good (God). Realizing the truth about our position in the Universe allows us to express our Joy.

These are a few of the infinite Values of Spirit that can be observed by studying the manifestations of Spirit. These Values are powerful and independent of our thinking, because Spirit expresses itself in the Universe by the Law of Its Being, independently of us. Spirit's being is its consciousness: its words are omniscient. Its Power is omnipotent and expressed by Universal Laws that are eternal with Spirit. There is no other way to be in the Universe than to fall under these Universal Laws.

No Other Options of Being Human

There are no new possibilities in the universe for being a human being; our options are set and we are born into them. Although the ways of being human are already present in the mind of man, there are really unlimited possibilities to manifest life as we know it. These unlimited possibilities exist because we are primarily spiritual beings that have human experiences. The fact is, an infinite variety of forms exist in the Universe. These forms have been and are being created by the Words of Spirit. And because of our true nature we have the ability to co-create with Spirit and help express the universe.

We Are the Creative Factor

To express the Universe there must be a co-creator. There are many things in the Universe that would not have been expressed had we not been created as spiritual beings endowed with concrete human experiences. This is our role as the Creative Factor and Co-creator in the universe. By choosing the words, thoughts, and feelings and expressing them uniquely, we fulfill our important role in the creative process.

Spirit did not create computers, automobiles, cell phones, etc., either in a vacuum or on its own. These, along with millions of other products that populate our world, need a co-creator. Such contributions exist because of the Creative Factor and the possibility of this is uniquely inherent within each of us. Without a co-creator, the Universe would be a very different place.

This is a very important point, which anyone can intuitively grasp simply by considering how different the

You Are To Your Life What Spirit Is To the Universe

Universe would have been without humanity co-creating with Spirit.

Imagine a universe without houses, computers, automobiles, airplanes, or even domestic animals and the thousands of wild animal and plant species that depend on the unique ecologies we co-create in our cities and countryside. There are so many things we have grown accustomed to through the ages. What if none of them were ever created by the word of Spirit and co-created by our unique expression of words, thoughts, and feelings? What would the Universe be like?

In one sense, I believe the universe would still be perfect, though not completely expressed. Without a co-creator capable of consciously tapping into the Spiritual Energy Field of All Possibilities (Spirit and Law) and using the creative gifts, it would not be the same, would it? The Universe would be missing something special.

Spirit may be the only Power that can move the stars by its word, but our words can move the stars in our lives. We rarely appreciate just how much our words can do this. If they didn't, the Universe Laws would operate without their full range of expression or possibilities.

Take the Law of Electricity. Imagine a world where we haven't yet discovered its application. That world existed only two centuries ago. Now imagine a world where we do not exist at all, where the mere possibility of co-creating the full range of expression of the Laws would be absurd. One might argue that there would still be lightning bolts in the sky. Lightning is only one form of electricity. It does not represent the full range of expression of the Law of Electricity. Therefore, something would be missing.

When you see this, you'll understand what is meant by the unity of all things.

Spirit Must Be a Unity

The substance of the Spiritual Energy Field of All Possibilities (Spirit and Law) is a unity. This point can be proven mathematically.

There cannot be two spirits, because Spirit is infinite. If we try to imagine two Spirits, we would soon find out that one Spirit would be limited by the other, which is absurd. You can't split the infinite. This is a point so fundamental that we simply must accept it. The infinite is a unity, as Thomas Troward had so elegantly proven through mathematics. It cannot be multiplied or divided. If it weren't so, mathematics itself would be invalid. Multiplying a unity would produce many units of the same size. Dividing it would produce many units of smaller size, to be sure. However, these units do not imply a unity at all, but multiplicity. We could go on and subdivide each unit into new units, ad infinitum.

There is no end. A unity is a single unit. Wherever it is it must be all there is.

The Co-creator

We now know that Spirit is a unity and constitutes the sole origin of the Universe and everything in it. From this, it logically follows that the creative process must start with a Universal Substance that is not manifested into any specific form. Moreover, it is merely the Spiritual Energy that we have proven to be a unity.

Before we ever speak our words as co-creators, we understand and see that the substance of Spirit is all the same. Until we provide a mold (a thought) for this Spiritual Substance, into which it can pour itself, there is only the unity or universal substance out of which everything is manifested.

You Are To Your Life What Spirit Is To the Universe

In order to create the Universe, this Substance must be everywhere present. It cannot be limited by space and time.

Only in this way is there such a thing as an individual expression of the Universe. We are all part of the unity of the Universe but different expressions of it.

So Who Are We, Really?

Asking this important question could help us develop our ability to move the stars in our lives, and in the process, provide an answer to the age-old question of why life is the way it is. Yet we must ask it within ourselves. We have to dig deep in our minds in order to give this question proper attention.

The best way I know to accomplish this is through meditation. By using only the conscious mind to pose this question, I expect to receive a variety of possible—though superficial—answers, such as:

- *I do not know who I am*
- *I am a good person*
- *I am a human being*
- *I am a child of God, and so on.*

These surface answers are no more than an attempt to resolve a deep-seated mystery that cannot be resolved on a conscious plane alone. The answer can only be experienced. The truth of the matter is we honestly have no conscious certainty who we really are, and any answer we come up with is rightly considered mere opinion, feeling, or some other passing sentiment.

The point is that we can only conclude that life resists easy answers. The best interpretation possible is the one you give it.

By way of example, think of a tree in the middle of a forest. If the tree is falling and there is no one in the forest to witness the event, did the tree really fall? How would you know for sure that it fell? The only way to know is to be there as a witness to the event.

This can only bring us to the conclusion that we, as human beings, give meaning to life through our interpretations of it. We interpret the events that happen to us. We do it in such a way as to acquire a point of view by which we could observe our life. In short, we give meaning to our life by our interpretations of life.

Therefore, let me ask you this: What is the particular perspective that allows you to interpret your life?

You Are a Spiritual Being

Once you understand that as human beings we give meaning to life by our own interpretation of life, you are ready to explore what we all do as spiritual beings. Spirituality is the other aspect of our nature whose central role is to be the Creative Factor and co-creator with Spirit in the Universe.

We Co-create Automatically

We co-create automatically in the Universe because spirituality is built into our nature. This does not mean that we are always aware of being co-creators. Most of the time we are not aware. Our subconscious mind has a creative power that does not question the instructions that we give it. Its only purpose is to manifest things based on a given pattern.

For example, you might unwittingly develop a consciousness of lack and limitation. Your subconscious mind is not going to tap you on the shoulder and ask if you really want to experience lack and limitation. It will follow your instruction to the letter and produce both.

Fortunately for most of us, we don't always have pure thoughts. Our thoughts are normally a mixture of good, bad, and not so bad. This mix is always present in the subconscious mind and distillates into a consciousness manifested in our life in the form of a pattern.

Just as Spirit is the creator of the heavens and the earth, so each of us is the co-creator of our lives. Spirit is perfect and always creates from Values. Spirit creates only a perfect manifestation. We have the opportunity to unify with the Values of Spirit and, by doing so; we raise our consciousness to a higher level. We can only accomplish this by being more in harmony with the Spiritual Energy Field of All Possibilities (Spirit and Law). This permits more of the creative energy to flow through us while allowing our higher consciousness to move the stars in our lives.

Speaking Your Words to Align With Spirit and Its Values

Here is how you can speak your words to align yourself with the Values and the omnipotence of Spirit:

> *I realize that I am one with pure Spirit. That Spirit is perfect in every way.*
>
> *I also know that the Values of Spirit are my values, and as I accept these Values into my life, I co-create*

abundance, joy and peace in everything I experience in my life.

There is neither doubt nor fear, because I know that I am rooted in pure Spirit. I have complete confidence in this creative energy, and know that it flows through every part of my being.

Since there is no limitation to the Law of Good in my life, Spirit is right where I am.

And so it is.

Your Words Work For You or Against You

–The Master Teacher once said:
By your words you are justified, by your words you are condemned.

You can move the stars in your life by tapping into the Spiritual Energy Field of All Possibilities (Spirit and Law). This energy field is the unity of all things seen and unseen. Because you have two aspects to your nature, you must learn how to work with both of them.

This is the only way you can move the stars in your life. You must co-create your individual life with Spirit as you give your life its meaning. This is another way of saying that you must discover how to speak your life into existence by the power of your words.

Co-creating Life

We help express the Universe by co-creating with Spirit. We can consciously tap into the Spiritual Energy Field of All Possibilities (Spirit and Law). Without our participation at that level of creation, the Universe would be radically different—and, as we saw, incomplete in its expression. Universal Laws operate independently; however without man and woman, neither the full expression nor even the possibility of full expression of the creative process would arise.

Moving the Stars With Your Words
Harold Davis, Msc.D., Ph.D

Human beings are able consciously to use Universal Laws, whether or not they go through life largely unaware of the awesome power they possess. The most vital aspect of our selves, our spirituality, makes us spiritual beings who have human experiences. It is important to understand the significance of this. We are neither just spiritual beings nor just physical beings. I have tried to impress this view upon everyone who has sought my advice.

Now, consider again the following question:
What is my role as a spiritual being?

Your answer by now should be, unequivocally:
My primary role as a spiritual being is to co-create

In this role, you discover Universal Laws and search for creative ways to express them in your daily life by being the Creative Factor. This is exactly what allows the Universe to find expression in the forms we observe.

However, there are better ways of expression than others. In short, there are bad choices and good choices.

Bad Choices

Human beings are very industrious, but industrious is not always wise. Clearly, many expressions of Universal Laws are not in our best interest. We frequently make grievously wrong choices. A prime example of bad choice is pollution. When we look around us, we find careless manufacturers polluting our natural environment as if there was no tomorrow.

Another example is the manner in which we modify the food we eat in ways that modify our bodily functions and fail to sustain the health of our physical bodies.

Witness also the destructive power of modern weaponry. We use it against one another, destroying human life, nature, and property.

I am sure you can think of numerous other examples of our ability to co-create for the destruction of life and the natural balance of Universal Laws. What is most disappointing about this kind of co-creation is that it is done out of greed for material things. We have received all the gifts we can imagine of the Spiritual Energy Field of All Possibilities (Spirit and Law), yet too many of us are blind to the truth—the truth that sets us free and allows us to leave a viable legacy for future generations.

Choice and Free Will

Choice allows us consciously to tap into the Spiritual Energy Field of All Possibilities (Spirit and Law) and thereby to raise the consciousness of the race. It is within our power to do this.

– *Harold Davis once said:*
> *Choice is a power we all possess, free will is the gift, but Law is the consequence*

Human powers alone are but an illusion, and a bigger illusion is that this is all we have. The sooner you own up to the reality of life, as it is active on three levels, the sooner you will begin to move the stars in your life. These three levels of activity are: the Spiritual, Mental, and Physical.

We live in a threefold Universe, where the body alone cannot create itself. The mind has to play an active role in this—as in every other—process, but creative energy flows directly from Spirit. Without this ultimate source of creative energy, nothing can be created.

Moving the Stars With Your Words
Harold Davis, Msc.D., Ph.D

Power Patterns in Your words

The patterns of our words produce positive and negative energies. Another way of expressing this is to say: By our words we are justified and by our words we are condemned.

Below is a list of words that create positive energy. Read it slowly in order to experience the energy in each word.

> **Giving**
> **Harmonious**
> **Powerful**
> **Orderly**
> **Optimistic**
> **Surrendering**
> **Tender**

Our words can produce negative energy as well. Read through the words below to experience how they contrast in energy with the above list:

> **Possessive**
> **Disruptive**
> **Forceful**
> **Confused**
> **Pessimistic**
> **Worrying**
> **Hard**

These negative words lie at the opposite ends of the energy scale compared to the first list. Any of them can be used in a sentence to create negative energy flow. Inserting words from the first list in the same sentence will immediately create positive flow of energy. This demonstrates the subtle power of the words that we speak. Once you add conscious thoughts and feelings to your expression of words, you will begin to move the stars in your life.

We Can Say "I am"

We have the capacity to act against our nature. The reason for this is that we can say "I am," and with this affirmation go on to define ourselves. Our subconscious mind then begins a creative process without questioning the request that emanates from this affirmation.

You can say "I am weak," "I am strong," "I am sick," or "I am healthy." Whatever you say about yourself will be created for you, because your words, thoughts, and feelings create your life conditions by forming a mold or thought-seed in your subconscious mind. Whether or not your affirmation corresponds to your true nature is an entirely different question that could have incalculable consequences in your life.

Through the Spiritual Energy Field of All Possibilities (Spirit and Law) we are connected in mind. Spirit creates a connection with every person. In doing so, it does something of utmost importance to us, not only as individuals but as members of society. Through this connection, it forms a coherent interpretation based on the way the majority of people interpret their lives.

This is unavoidable. It is how we recognize each other, communicate, and share experiences. Without it we are like solitary atoms or dust particles blowing in whatever direction the wind happens to be moving, no different from any inanimate object.

Moving the Stars With Your Words
Harold Davis, Msc.D., Ph.D

Our Words Create Movement in Mind

Each word, thought, and feeling creates a vibration within us that activates our creative power. When we speak our words, things start to happen in mind. This is called **the Law of Mind in Action.**

Below is a list of characteristics associated with words. Read them carefully at least once and try to relate them to your own life.

> *The word fills the immediate atmosphere with an unseen vibration.*
>
> *The word is a vibration in the mind.*
>
> *The word affects the physical atmosphere in which it is spoken.*
>
> *The word affects human beings, animals, plants, and inanimate objects.*
>
> *The word is a vibration of energy that draws to itself that which is of like nature, whether positive or negative.*
>
> *The word gives rise to a vibration that is in direct proportion to the intensity of the feelings with which it is spoken.*
>
> *The word either clears or clouds the atmosphere.*
>
> *The word creates healing vibrations throughout our bodies if it is positive in its nature.*

The word creates a destructive vibration throughout our bodies, if it is negative in its nature.

By realizing and experiencing the power in the characteristics associated with the words you speak, you will begin to realize your power to move the stars in your life.

Realizing Power

We realize creative results only to the degree that our words, thoughts, and feelings are in harmony with Spirit. The flow of creative energy through us is always in direct proportion to the flow of spiritual energy, and the conviction behind the particular words, thoughts, feelings expresses what we want or don't want.

You are always co-creating something in your life, because creative energy never ceases to flow and we never stop thinking and believing in something. This is one of those options we were born into and cannot change. You should determine the words that you wish to speak, because these words, thoughts, and feelings are what determine your experiences.

To make full use of your power to move the stars with your words, you must identify with Spirit, keep a clear concept (words, thoughts, and feelings) about what you want, and strengthen your conviction to experience what you want.

Be, Do, and Have

Our words, thoughts, and feelings are the seeds that bring forth what we want to experience. You can Be in the universe, and manifest what you want from the Spiritual Energy Field of All Possibilities (Spirit and Law) by being true to yourself.

Moving the Stars With Your Words
Harold Davis, Msc.D., Ph.D

It is commonly believed that we must Have something, in order to Do something, and only then can we Be something. If this is how you've been thinking about the creative process, then you are conjuring up the concepts of Having, Doing, and Being in the wrong sense. You are attempting to use the creative process in reverse.

In reality, we don't have to have anything, because everything is created from the Spiritual Energy Field of All Possibilities (Spirit and Law). We don't have to do anything to be successful, because everything is created in the mind first; the gifts have already been bestowed upon us.

Instead of having and doing in order to be, you must first Be. It's primordial, and the only thing required of you. After that, you can do and have whatever you want to experience in your life. If you can be joyful, if you can be loving, if you can be prosperous, if you can be persistent and consistent in your every thought, then you will do and have whatever you truly desire.

I assure you, this is the paradigm that will absolutely transform your life.

Let me put it in the terms we established in the earlier example of the carrot seeds. When a farmer plants carrot seeds, what does he expect to harvest in the future once the plant matures?

Nothing but carrots, of course!

If a watermelon should grow instead of a carrot, he'd be in serious trouble, because either he has planted the wrong seed or a major Law has been altered beyond recognition. While we can envision circumstances where human oversight is the culprit reason that leads to the first possibility, we cannot imagine how a carrot seed could possibly yield a watermelon.

Question
Since the carrot-seed example is still fresh in our memory, let's try to recall what we said before we move forward.

How does a carrot seed become a carrot?

A carrot seed contains all the information it needs to become a carrot, but the soil acts as the substance that transforms this information into a carrot. I am not saying that the soil decides what that seed ought to become. There is a big difference.

My point is that words are like seeds. What we believe, feel, and think generates the information we know as a word. The good news is that the word does not decide anything. We have the ability to decide what we want to co-create. After all, that is exactly what our role and purpose is: to co-create.

Moreover, we can change our words, thoughts, feelings, and beliefs to suit different purposes, and in so doing, change what we originally intended to manifest—sometimes without even knowing it. One minute we might be thinking about the possibility of manifesting an abundant life, the next minute something negative happens that sets us off on a tangent and we start thinking only about the life of deprivation and limitation that we are experiencing.

You have probably done this. One minute you're thinking something, the next another. Now, just extrapolate those two minutes in your waking day onto the tapestry of a whole lifetime and you will understand how a change in thinking can permanently alter the direction of one's life.

Whether we're speaking in terms of minutes or years, you always have the power to re-invent yourself. You can change your experience at any time, no matter what the circumstances.

This is what I mean by the power of choice. It is a power that guarantees success and happiness, even when the conditions are not what they could be or what we want them to be. No matter what your present experience, there is at least one thing you can do that nothing in this world can rob you of: changing your life by changing your words.

Take a person whose dream is to be a millionaire. The normal definition of a millionaire is anyone who has a million dollars in the bank. That alone earns him the title of millionaire. The trouble is that while this may be true by strict definition, that person will never be a millionaire in his experience until he becomes a millionaire in his mind.

The good news is that everyone is a millionaire in Spirit to begin with; therefore, you would need only the consciousness of prosperity you associate with being a millionaire to attract to yourself the right people, circumstances, and conditions to co-create exactly this type of wealth.

Walking by Faith, Not by Sight

"To be or not to be," said the man who more than anyone else in history shaped the English language. William Shakespeare had an unmatched genius for both language and the human sentiments he portrayed in his plays and poems. His characters expressed the full range of feelings and thoughts. They were not static objects that merely decorated the stage, but loving, hating, dreaming, or avenging individuals with thoughts that transformed them and the world around them.

To transform your life you must have faith. To Be, you must walk by faith not by sight. You should turn away from the unwanted conditions that impact your life. They do not have the consciousness to act on their own. They are not unbidden. They emanate from the secondary causes you have conjured up yourself.

Turn toward Spirit and speak what you want with conviction and faith (that is, feeling and belief). When you do this, you plant the seeds of success in your mental garden. Then use your will power to focus your conscious thought. Let it take root in the fertile soil of your subconscious mind, which is the creative medium of the Universe. Your words, thoughts, and feelings provide the form that produces your Being. Your subconscious mind provides the Law that creates what you want to manifest in mind from whatever form you provide by Being.

If you want abundance, you must Be abundant in mind. If you want to have perfect health, you must Be healthy in mind. You are the seed, so stay true to the experiences you want to Have. You cannot Have this experience or Do the activities for its manifestation until you become it.

To summarize, the Law of Mind in Action creates from the information you provide to it by simply becoming what you become in your mind's eye. Then, and only then, will the Spirit move the stars toward the good you most cherish.

The Truth Sets Us Free

The "knowledge" I have alluded to is whatever we have been searching for all of our lives. This is the knowledge that will free us to live out our dream. It frees us for life. This is what I am seeking to convey in this chapter.

Most of us keep searching for this knowledge within the limited options of the physical universe. Sometimes we imagine finding it. Now we know that this is an illusion. All truth can only be found within us. We know it is not people, not the economy, not the conditions of life, and nothing outside ourselves.

None of these things will allow you to live your dream. Only your power of choice can do that.

This is all about our power to be what we want to be by saying two simple but powerful words: I am. It is the truth that sets us free to live our dreams and be the person we want to be.

Will Power as a Powerful Tool

Will is the means by which we take back control of our lives. Without Will, our life is not self-directing but is being directed from outside of ourselves.

It need not be so. You have the ability to take command of your life and its direction simply by willing the things you want. Will is the inescapable element of action you need to mount an offensive on your subconscious mind's control center.

Start by assuming that the Will is an agent of the spirit. As a spiritual being, you are capable of incredible feats. What most people end up accomplishing is paltry and disappointing compared to what they are capable of.

After that, develop your will; train it to select the kind of actions that promise to produce the results you want. Your Will must remain active in your spirit. It directs your words, thoughts, and feelings.

What is Will?
For a fuller understanding of Will, you need an accurate description. There are several ways of defining will, but essentially it must contain four elements active in the mind: **Will as the Mind Controller, Focus Controller, Desire Controller, and Belief Controller.**

Mind Controller.
Let's first examine the Will as an element of the mind that controls. In this respect, it determines how we experience our life. This is how the Will is mostly experienced.

Now, take it a step higher.

Will also helps shape your personality; it is the agent that determines how you interface with people, things, and how you see life in general. Will ensures your persistence of mind. We have all heard of the role that persistence plays in personal success. It is the sign of a strong Will to accomplish a task that either your Will power or faith has chosen.

Focus Controller.
Will is also the element of mind that operates as the controller of focus. It is up to Will to determine the direction of your mental focus. Without this trait, you are doomed to wonder aimlessly through the valleys and peaks of life. Will focuses thoughts in a direction of your own choosing and allows you to keep your word seed in the mental soil of the mind long enough to produce the results that you want to experience.

Desire Controller.
Another way that Will operates as an element of the mind is as the controller of desire. Due to its compelling nature, desire has a major impact on how our life plays itself out. If you use your will to direct thoughts in a way that generates the effects you desire, then the main fruit of your labors should be a life lived with passion. It should be filled with great, enriching experiences.

Belief Controller.
Will is also an element of mind that operates as the controller of beliefs. Beliefs determine how you interpret things you encounter in the world. You can believe in a brighter future, or

you can believe that neither the world nor your future has anything to offer other than what you've already received in the past.

If you currently enjoy the good fruits of your thoughts, perhaps you don't see the need to change or redirect your beliefs through will and thought. In the end, only you can decide whether or not the beliefs that you have can bring you success in the future.

The Three Levels of Will

In addition to the four aspects of will that we just talked about, there are three significant levels of Will: **Highest Will, Average Will, and Zero Will.**

Highest Will.
The three significant levels of will have a unique effect on your mind, but at different times in your life. Highest will is the level that you should strive to experience. From this level, you can gain mastery of your conscious mind through the power of your words. Highest will is the highest form of the Will we are capable of experiencing, so this is the level you ought to experience as often as possible. At this level, we have an open path directly from the Spiritual Energy Field of All Possibilities (Spirit and Law) that gives our expression maximum power.

Can you remember a time when everything was working perfectly in your life? You were on a roll and nothing could stand in your way. You felt unstoppable. The answers to complex mental challenges came to you in flashes of inspiration. Even physical obstacles were easily overcome. It was just one of those rare moments in life when you were in flow and your conscious mind was being directed by the Will at its highest level.

If you can remember such a moment, you will certainly appreciate how it felt to maintain a constant level of ease. For most people, it is a rare experience indeed, though it doesn't have to be this way.

Most of the time, Will is too weak to produce the desired results, but it is always available to you. Your will can be trained to function more consistently, but you must exercise it until it is strong enough to maintain itself at a constant high level. To develop will, you must start with the level of control you presently have over it. From that level, you can start building on what you have. From the weaker you can build a stronger Will. Cultivating your personal will power is similar to building the muscles in your body.

The fact is that we all have Will, but some of us have not yet determined when and how to use it. When we gain control of our Will, we allow it to be consistent. It gives us more precision to co-create the effects we want in our life.

To illustrate the exercise of Will, think of the desire to go out shopping at the mall for a new pair of shoes. If you really want this to happen, all you have to do is turn your desire into will power and will your conscious mind to instruct your body to take action.

We do this every time we want something. But lack of motivation sometimes impinges on our will power and we end up with a weak drive that keeps us from achieving our aim.

If you take charge of your body through the power of the conscious mind, you will be motivated to accomplish any task you choose. You can achieve this simply by choosing to do it and by staying focused on the task in hand.

Average Will.
Average will is where the will operates at the level of the collective though of the human race. Will at this level has begun to show signs of making healthy choices, however inconsistently. One may look at it as the level of will at which a person is able to reflect on who he or she is. This ability allows you to see yourself as separate from one's personality.

Zero Will.
Zero is the level at which there is no will. Here, will is completely missing from the equation and the person is subjugated to whatever conditions he has attracted. That person is clearly a victim of his circumstances.

It may sound extreme, but many people in our society experience this level of will. A good example is someone who has lost the will to live. At that level, there is very little conscious energy present. The only conscious energy available is the product of shame, guilt, and apathy. Such a level imparts a life-depleting energy that fosters a hopeless or nearly hopeless life view, where the will is completely inactive.

Desire

What do you want to experience in life?

If you are like most people, you probably haven't given it much thought. Maybe you're so confused about what you want from life that you associate thinking itself with pain.

The only way to overcome this condition as painlessly as possible is to focus on what you desire to experience in your life. Don't leave it to chance. You must paint a picture of the promise in your mind's eye. We fail to focus on what we want because we get caught up trying to earn a living. Life's mundane tasks take up so much personal energy that we fail to decide exactly what we want to experience. In the end, we prefer to keep our thoughts superficial and general. Inevitably, however, the negative experiences in life catch up with us.

Take the person who constantly thinks about what isn't working in his life. Such a person will never be able to change the negative conditions in his life, because he is blinded by an ongoing problem. At one point, it becomes a self-fulfilling prophecy for the simple reason that his single-minded focus on the negative is the problem. He has never taken the opportunity to plant a thought-seed aligned with his true vision or desire.

If you are serious about moving the stars in your life, you must understand that focus is the single controlling activity that determines what you experience in life. If you desire love, then you must have love as your focus. It is important that you keep your focus as a matter of course.

I suggest that you make a shortlist of about four to six areas of your life on which you want to focus. These areas should be, at a minimum, your health consciousness, prosperity consciousness, social consciousness, spiritual consciousness, and a couple more areas of consciousness you feel are important. This step alone will multiply the successes in your life.

Your focus on the experience in your consciousness is the key to building a strong thought atmosphere—through you, around you, and one that flows from you.

Thought Atmosphere

The less control you have over your own thought atmosphere, the more people around you will affect you. Conversely, you can have a positive effect on the quality of your life and that of others by cultivating a strong thought atmosphere.

Your ability to focus your thoughts is the key to accomplishing this.

You can create a strong thought atmosphere by building strong consciousness in an area of your life you consider most important. If you're around people who are always complaining about life, your thought atmosphere will be weak and vulnerable to their negative thoughts. Conversely, if you lack focus and purpose, you will adopt some of the same thought patterns you find around you.

The focus on what you want is vitally important to your success. It will allow your mind to maintain subconscious control of the body, which in turn produces the physical actions needed to accomplish the goals you set at the proper level of consciousness.

What Causes Human Problems?

Personally, the interpretations I derive give meaning to my life. The flip side of this is that they can deplete my life of meaning, too. I'm not one to lay the blame for my misfortunes except where blame belongs: Me.

I am the principal cause of my problems.

This may not be the most widely accepted view of personal responsibility. Many people are loath to accept it in the face of the sorry conditions they find themselves in. It's always more comforting to heap blame on everything and everyone else. We do it all the time, forgetting that the opposite of this is actually the better news.

If you take the time to analyze this, you will discover just how good the news is!

When I say that I am to blame for my mistake, I am not destined to suffer for that mistake because a supreme being is meting out punishment. We suffer for our mistakes because of the bad choices we make with our own free will, and because the Law of Cause and Effect will take effect automatically.

Most choices we make are more or less based on circumstances, where the information is either incomplete or too static to assist in proper decision-making. This is especially true in critical situations, where we don't have the luxury of picking through the information at will, and knowing the root cause of the situation. When the situation is not of a critical nature, the outcome may have none, or less, of the adverse impact. Instead, we are influenced by the cumulative effects of all the small choices we have made in the past. The collective pattern and accumulation of these choices spawn the undesirable results manifesting themselves in our lives. One small error in judgment can cause our lives to head down the wrong path. Likewise, the right choice can cause a better outcome.

There is a better way for you to experience life and make better choices. You can live life from the inside out, or you can live it from the outside in. The best example I can think of is that of the master-teacher, when he said to his pupil, "Walk by faith and not by sight."

Stop living life from the outside in.

Points of Perception

For a powerful representation of how we can relate to our life and how we actually live that life, think of different points of perception. These points ultimately reveal what we perceive as our source of power: **Spiritual Perception, Perception of Values, Perception of Identity, Perception of Beliefs,**

Perception of Capabilities, Perception of Actions, and Perception of Conditions.

These perception points can serve as a framework for discovering how you currently co-create your life and how to make adjustments to this process if need be or if you desire it.

Spiritual Perception.

Everything comes from this point, including you. It denotes the Spiritual Energy Field of All Possibilities, and by definition, it is Omnipotent (all the power there is), Omniscient (all the knowledge there is), and Omnipresent (everywhere present). You should perceive that you are a spirit in The Spirit, a spiritual being that has human experiences.

Perception of Values.

This point represents the Values of Spirit. In chapter 3, I discussed a few of the Values of Spirit, and explained how they could have a very powerful effect on your ability to co-create what you really want in your life. Review those values again, because what you need to do is adopt them in your life.

Perception of Identity.

At the identity point, what usually shows up is your basic sense of self, your personality, and your ego. It is part of being human. However, at this level you have the ability to identify with your real self (Spirit and Law). That's the choice you ought to make. The real self is who you really are, and your perception of it is the source of your power. When you identify yourself with the ego, you will see how the source of your power is made up of all the things manifested in your life, and is directly related to time and space. It might be your health, money, and affairs. Most of your success depends on how you wield your real power, not the will power itself, which is not the real power.

Perception of Beliefs.
At this perception point, you have already developed concepts about your life that you trust and on which you rely for your daily activity. These concepts can stand for both limitation and permission. A belief is only what imparts a feeling of certainty about something or what it means. It may stem from a source of knowledge with which you're familiar or a source of illusion. When that source is derived from external results only, you can be pretty certain it has an illusion attached to it. This can cause you to co-create lack and limitation in your life.

Perception of Capabilities.
At this point of perception, you can avail yourself of certain categories of actions, skills, and strategies in your daily life. Proper use of capabilities requires motivation or inspiration, which may result from either the deep-seated beliefs you happen to entertain or the collective opinions of the human race. One thing I found to be true of most people is that they will use their capabilities primarily either to gain the experiences that they want or to avoid the ones that they don't want. It is unfortunate that people spend more time trying to avoid the experiences they co-create rather than enjoy the real pleasures of life they could co-create, if they really set themselves to it.

Perception of Actions.
At the action point, you engage in the type of behavior either that best corresponds with your capabilities or regardless of them. Your interpretation of the present conditions may be a negative or positive force. It all depends on whether or not it is truthful to who you really are and what you really want. The

wrong interpretation may drive you—again, like the majority of people—to do more to avoid what you don't want rather than to go for what you want in life. This is part and parcel of the human condition, which you can choose to rise above.

Perception of Conditions.
The condition or effect point of perception contains what most people react to: the environment, the people they meet, and the basic patterns of the observed Universe. All of these constitute your life experiences, which you have co-created from speaking your words, your thoughts, your feelings. Inside, you have the ability to control every condition, because conditions are not things of themselves. They have no power beyond what you give them. A condition has no will of its own that enables it to interfere with your life. It is not a thing in itself, but a no-thing.

The Perception of Co-creating Conditions

There are two basic ways of co-creating conditions in your life. Eighty-five percent of people on this planet co-create their lives from the outside in (object-referring), only fifteen percent co-create their lives from the inside out (real self-referring). My percentages may not be exact, and some people may use a combination of the two, but you get the picture. The vast majority co-create derivatives of the effects that influence their lives, nothing more.

Creating Life From Effect

Being object-referring, or acting from effect, gives a particular orientation to the flow of will power. This is how most people co-create their lives. By living life as an object-referring person you will soon find that your conditions are determining your actions. By reacting to the conditions of your life, you are forced to take specific actions based on a habitual pattern, and these actions in turn determine the habitual capabilities you develop and use in the future.

Habitual capabilities influence beliefs about the conditions and about the self. They decide what you believe about yourself and how you identity yourself in relation to any given condition. Therefore, their impact is huge.

This way of living life works so long as the condition or event remains positive. Obviously, this is not always the case. Some negative condition or event will eventually impinge on your life that calls for a less than ideal response within the subconscious mind. Your identity will then create a set of values which you will continue to live by long after the condition or event has vanished, or until some other effect changes your mind and, thereby, your values.

Your self-image in all of this is critical to the way you live.

Conditions are like the blowing of the wind; their direction is constantly shifting, and they change in tandem with the change of words, thoughts, and feelings. A change in the conditions may alter your beliefs about life. Since your words, thoughts, and feelings are like seeds, you will inevitably experience that change in whatever is being co-created for you. But while a carrot seed remains constant, your thought-seed has the ability to change for better or worst. So, no one is completely helpless.

There is always hope, if you can refrain from victimizing yourself. Living your life from the self-perception I call object-referring, you will remain a victim of unpredictable secondary causes, never able to change for the better. It is impossible for anyone to predict the truth that secondary causes hide or what really needs to be done to deal with them if the conditions and circumstances being interpreted are not the original knowledge that should determine the course of your life.

The truth behind a thought-pattern has its origin from Spirit or first cause. This thought-pattern should result from your words, thoughts, and feelings.

Remember the earlier analogy we used, where the visible part of the iceberg represented consciousness? The conditions you see about you make up the iceberg observable above the surface, beneath which lies the rest of it, the actual size and depth, and these are impossible to judge. What I mean to say is that you cannot determine the total truth about secondary causation, and this contributes to the uncertainty of an object-referring life.

All first causes occur at a spiritual level, not at the conditional level. This is where our connection to the Spiritual Energy Field of All Possibilities (Spirit and Law) becomes very important. The best orientation you can have for your life is when you live according to the perception of being self-referring, from inside out.

Co-creating Life from Spirit

Real self-referring is from Spirit. It signifies the orientation of the flow of real power. After all, spirit can do for us only what it does through us. We know by now that Spirit is within us, not out there somewhere. By being real self-referring, you employ real power.

You must identify with your spiritual nature and adopt Spirit's Values. Try to recall some of the observable values I mentioned earlier: Unconditional Love, Wisdom, Peace, Joy, Abundance, Power, etc. By identifying with the source of all power, your identity will be in complete harmony with Spirit, and if you are in true harmony with Spirit, you will be able to adopt its Values.

Belief in yourself will be strong because of the strong self-image that develops from a perception based on your conscious relationship with Spirit. This will allow you to respond productively to conditions and events in a way that ensures the best manifested results. You will speak the results that you desire most to co-create. It doesn't matter if the problem assailing you has to do with health, finance, or some other life issue. Spirit will take the words that you speak and turn them into an exact copy in your life.

Living your life from the perception of being real self-referring allows you to be the Creative Factor in your life. It matters little what is going on in the physical universe around you. You become to your life what Spirit is to the Universe. You become the Creative Factor in your life, a co-creator with Spirit.

Power Patterns in Your words

The patterns of your words produce a positive energy and a negative energy. Another way of expressing this is to say: "By our words we are justified and by our words we are condemned."

Now look again at the list of positive and negative words you saw earlier. You learned that these words created positive and negative energy within us depending on the word spoken. This time I have placed them side by side in order to contrast their energy. Read them slowly, and feel the contrast of the positive or negative energy of each word.

       Giving / Possessive
       Harmonious / Disruptive

Moving the Stars With Your Words
Harold Davis, Msc.D., Ph.D

> Powerful / Forceful
> Orderly / Confused
> Optimistic / Pessimistic
> Surrendering / Worrying
> Tender / Hard

This exercise of speaking your words will enable you to control the flow of creative energy that flows through you, around you, and from you.

How Spirit Works Through Us

The statement "Let Go, Let Spirit" is true in every sense. Most people are unwilling to let go of their false sense of security, and unaware that the truth of these powerful words would set them free. Having the faith to trust in our higher power is a real challenge, there's no question, and yet the only way we can use this power is by letting Spirit work through us.

But what does letting go really mean?

First and foremost, it means that you avoid trying to concentrate or hold on to thoughts. Letting go rests on the will power to co-create what you want by being in complete harmony with Spirit. You are Spirit's instrument, by which new things are created and manifested into the mental and physical universe.

Alone you create nothing at all. You can only co-create. "It is not I but my father within me that do the work" — in other words, Spirit. By the same token, it is not the concentration or will power that works, but the consciousness behind your words.

These teachings have been repeated over the centuries, sadly without always being understood. By letting go of your effort to control everything, you let the highest power work through you. To be effective at this, you must be in a state of unity with Spirit, in complete harmony with it. Only then will you be able to direct the flow of creative energy through you by words, thoughts, and feelings.

Allow your consciousness to rise. Let it vibrate at a level that attracts your desired good into your mind, body, and affairs. You will quickly see how your dreams are made manifest by the expression behind your words, and how the stars in your life are moved.

Speaking Your Words for Your Highest Good

Here is an example of how you can speak your words to co-create your highest good and negate those conditions which are not in your best interest:

> *I realize that I am created from pure Spirit, and that my Spiritual nature is in complete harmony with Spirit.*
>
> *I maintain an orientation with Spirit that always allows me to co-create my life from the inside out, which is from a perception of real self-referring.*
>
> *Therefore, I always co-create the conditions, and experiences that I want to have in my life. I know that lack and limitation are a lie. They are false evidence that only appears to be real, the result of giving power to the outside world of effect.*
>
> *I have complete confidence in Spirit and know that it is flowing through every part of my being.*

Spirit is now working for my highest good and the highest good of the human race. This is the truth about life, the whole truth, and nothing but the truth.

And so it is...

The Impact of Relative Filters on Your Words

– Leo Buscaglia once said:
> Time has no meaning in itself unless we choose to give it significance.

We often fail to move and achieve what society regards as the basic necessities in our lives. So, it's not surprising that the average person doesn't even consider moving the stars in his or her life a possibility. The average person will let opportunities past by, and not bother to take advantage of the opportunity that life really is. In general, we lack the vision and faith in our ability to succeed, even in the face of serious challenges. We usually fall victim to the appearance of the situation, and to time itself.

In the previous chapter, you discovered that your words have the ability to release creative energy, and that if you live your life by being real self-referring you will direct the full flow of this energy for your benefit.

In this chapter, you will discover why the ability to perceive time from different perspectives is a very important mental skill. You will also discover that time itself is a mental construct, and that it is only relative to us as human beings and not as spiritual beings. I will show you how past conditions, the collective unconsciousness of the human race, and the present conditions can restrict the full flow of creative energy through and from you.

Perception of Time

Your time perception begins with the starting point of a journey that will bring you face-to-face with your destiny.

You need to examine your starting point.

One way to do this is by examining the position you occupy in your personal timeline—namely, the representation of events occurring within linear time. Imagine a personal timeline that represents the linear course of your life. The five time relationships that are a part of your personal timeline are: pre-birth, past, present, future, and afterlife.

Your personal timeline began inside your mother's womb, before you were ever born. It stretches from conception to the present and into the future. Between the two extremes lie your perceptions of the past and of the possibilities of the future. However, the only point where you can have a personal impact is in the elusive present. Your present is always shifting toward the future.

Note how your personal timeline is arranged in your mind's eye. Try to develop a mental representation of the timeline. You can do this by using your imagination. There are two common ways in which human beings represent time in their mind: in-time (back-front) and through-time (side-to-side) representation.

In-Time.
If you tend toward a representation in terms of a back-front or in-time timeline, then that mental time arrangement suits you best for defining your Vision, Mission, and Purpose in life. This time arrangement allows you to be in the moment more often, which is the point of maximum creative energy.

Through-Time.
If you discover that time is best represented side-to-side or through time, then this is the mental time arrangement that best allows you to observe your past and future. By looking to your left for the past and looking to your right for the future, you can continually monitor these two time dimensions (past and future). In some cases, where a person is left-handed the direction of past and future is reversed. This time arrangement will help you set goals and implement them through time.

Where Are Your Past and Future?

For many people, the past produces a dragging effect. This indicates an in-time timeline arrangement. Their future is in front of them, but they carry all their baggage from the past wherever they go.

The problem with this arrangement of past and future is this. The past is always hidden from view, so the only way for them to learn from the past is to look back; however, they prefer not to. They much rather gaze into the future and pray for a break. This is one way to cope that offers hope for a brighter tomorrow. They unconsciously arrange their timeline in this fashion because they often harbor memories of painful events from their past and perceive the present as an extension of their past.

Rearrange Your Past and Future for Impact

If you have an in-time arrangement, try placing your past to your left and your future to the right (you may reverse this direction if you prefer). It is helpful to learn from the past in order to avoid repeating the same mistakes.

Life is a hard teacher. If you fail to learn from the past, your life will keep giving you hard lessons, over and over, until your consciousness rises. Life will go on relentlessly at this pace until you learn the lessons it teaches.

The present is constantly shifting into the future, but the future is best placed to the right (to the left if you preferred to reverse the direction of this model). If you have a compelling future with big goals and dreams with a clear path, then it will pull you toward it like a giant magnet. This is the Law of Intention and Desire at work.

You will accomplish none of your goals and dreams if you cannot see the illusion and change your way of thinking. Your life will simply conform to the statistical trends of so many others who have come before you, and you'll wonder why you haven't achieved your dreams.

From this brief description of linear timelines, you can see the benefits in both In-Time and Through-Time representations. I recommend that you master both types in your mind. This skill will help you work within your mind's eye, focus your consciousness, and build a higher level of consciousness.

Keep in mind that time is no more than a mental construct that exists only in reference to something else and is, therefore, an illusion. The only point of power on your timeline is the "now." Every other point is mere illusion. Only the present moment is real.

The Illusion of Time

While the only point on your personal timeline where you can exercise personal power is the present moment, the present is endlessly shifting into the future. You may try to predict that future or to change the past, but all you can

The Impact of Relative Filters on Your Words

succeed in doing is influencing future events by what you do now.

Still, the past is a part of your personal timeline. It represents events that have already taken place. Many people become fixated with the past. They focus on their past as if it were possible to alter what has already taken place. I don't need to tell you that no one can tinker with past events. But while this is no doubt true, you can still change how past events affect you in the present.

I once had the opportunity to work with a client, whom I will call Ann. She had been bitter toward men for most of her adult life, but she did not consciously know why her intimate relationships always seemed to end prematurely because of some unfounded suspicion she had about her mate. She would vividly imagine her mate to be in a clandestine love affair with another woman.

After working with her for no more than a half-hour, I discovered that she had an unresolved issue with her father. Thirty years earlier she had inadvertently discovered her father carrying on an affair with another woman. She confronted him about his infidelity, and a big argument ensued. To make a long story short, Ann had never forgiven her father for his mistake, even after thirty years. I told her about the power of forgiveness and the benefit of letting go of the past. Ann was able to see how her past was affecting her, and was willing to forgive her father. In fact, she was able to speak with him over the phone after making a few calls. She was able to let him know, among other things, that she had forgiven him. She also asked for his forgiveness, and they started a new relationship based on the consciousness forgiveness.

Needless to say, her health and current marital relationship are now at an all time high. She was able to let go of all the negative emotions she had been lugging around

Moving the Stars With Your Words
Harold Davis, Msc.D., Ph.D

inside her mental storehouse for so long. A great weight was lifted off her shoulders. New and exciting things started showing up in her life—she was a new woman.

Ann's story illustrates how past interpretations can hurt us. You, too, can learn to reframe the past by using it as a reference tool. It could help you co-create a better future. The future is not here yet. As a matter of fact, we never quite arrive in the future. Your future is right now in the present. You can create a vision of it that is compelling for you and that will inspire you to speak your words with conviction.

Use the past only to contrast it with your vision of the present. It will help you develop a compelling future based on your desires. But you also have the ability to develop a future that is not based on any memory-stored event, without reference to the past and based only on your imagination or vision.

Thanks to this powerful ability, your thoughts can and will become the things you imagine them to be. Imagine what it would be like to develop your future, without perceived limitations.

Do you remember the famous track star Rodger Banister? He was the first man to run a sub-four-minute mile. Before he accomplished this magnificent feat, the experts believed it was impossible. Of course, for anyone who thought this way, it could only be impossible. But Rodger succeeded, and hundreds of others followed in his footsteps. The best time ever recorded now stands somewhere below three minutes forty-eight seconds. There are high school milers who routinely run well below the four-minute-mile mark.

The Three Relative Filters in Your Life

Spirit can only do for us what it can through us. But there are filters that restrict its flow through us, around us, and from us. These filters do not change or affect Spirit in any way. Spirit is absolute in its nature and by definition subject to nothing. These filters are all relative and become our reference point in the creative process we choose to be part of.

Relative Filters become our reference because of the poor actions we tend to perform in disregard of our power of choice. Consequently, they block our flow of creative energy. To understand how these relative filters block creative energy, we must refer to the Law of Relativity.

According to the Law of Relativity, because we are finite beings, we live relative to some part of the Universe. Spirit, on the other hand, is absolute in its nature and is relative to nothing else; it is infinite and omnipresent; it created the Universe out of itself. Since we are relative by our very nature, the choices we make can prevent us from creating what we claim we want. They do this by altering the flow of creative energy through us.

There are three kinds of relative filters that can partially block the creative energy that flows through us: **Personal History, Collective Unconsciousness, and Present Conditions.**

Personal History.
Personal History comprises the events, stories and perceptions you have experienced since birth. If the majority of these experiences are positive, then the perspective you adopt will allow more of the creative energy to flow freely through you. If the majority is negative, your Personal History will restrict your flow of creative energy.

Moving the Stars With Your Words
Harold Davis, Msc.D., Ph.D

Collective Unconsciousness.
The term Collective Unconsciousness denotes the collective interpretations of all Human Beliefs. These interpretations may be either true or false, but we are all in one mind — this is how we recognize each other, share experiences, and perceive events that happen in the universe.

The flow of creative energy is greater when the collective thoughts are positive than when they are negative. Phrased differently, the flow of creative energy depends on the degree to which the collective thought is colored by the truth.

In the distant past, when our collective thought rested on the view that the world was flat, it kept us in bondage, and this bondage prevented the human race from exploring the earth to its farthest reaches. The human race was not free to explore the earth without fear of falling off the edge. It was an illusion that ultimately had to be challenged and the truth was revealed.

This example brings to mind a research project I once read about that began around 1952 and lasted over thirty years. The scientists were studying the behavior of a colony of monkeys on an island. As an experiment, they provided raw sweet potatoes as a new addition to the monkey's diet. The monkeys liked the taste of the sweet potatoes, but they found the dirt unpleasant. One young female discovered that she could remove the unpleasant taste of the dirt by washing the sweet potatoes in a stream. She taught her mother and a few other monkeys in her colony how to wash the sweet potatoes. By the autumn of 1958, the scientists were observing a certain number of other monkeys washing sweet potatoes in the stream. Clearly, this new skill had been passed on to them.

But then an amazing event took place. After one additional monkey on the island was taught to wash the sweet potatoes, all the others began to wash sweet potatoes before eating them. The added mental energy of this additional monkey seemed to have broken through some sort of collective barrier.

The scientists were utterly surprised by this behavior. The monkeys had actually experienced a paradigm shift. Amazingly, the act of washing the sweet potatoes crossed over to the colonies on other islands that had no physical contact with the original colony of monkeys!

This is hard to explain without reference to the notion of critical mass. It took a certain number of monkeys to reach a critical mass of awareness, which was then communicated from mind to mind. Although the exact number needed to achieve critical mass in that colony of monkeys is unknown, and may vary from experiment to experiment, the researchers dubbed this the Hundredth Monkey Phenomenon.

This implies that a limited number of people could become aware of something through mind that is their exclusive conscious property, until a point called critical mass is reached. As the point of new awareness, Critical Mass strengthens the energy field in mind, allowing the information to be received by everyone open to receiving the information! This research deepens our insight into how and why human evolution takes place. The insight can be especially valuable when the information in mind is received directly from first cause, or Spirit. However, if the information is based on a false opinion, it will restrict the flow of spiritual energy through the collective. This is reflected in the Law of Averages and may be used to predict the success or failure of an action, project, or a group of people.

Interpretation of Present Conditions.
Present Conditions are interpreted with the intent of obtaining the truth of a condition, which is always of a secondary nature. I have covered this point in detail earlier in this book. A secondary source of information is always incomplete, not

unlike the visible part of the iceberg in relation to the mass that lies hidden underneath. We can always guess the approximate mass below with certain calculations, but operating from incomplete knowledge only through sight, hearing, taste, smell, and touch is insufficient. The information obtained from the outer senses is of a secondary nature and often unreliable.

The conditions we sense from the relative perspective of the three relative filters are no different—they are mere illusions. The interpretations we derive through these filters restrict the creative energy that flows through us.

In truth, there is nothing between spirit and us; it is we who place these filters by identifying with extraneous sources of information. The more we identify with relative sources, the more we restrict the flow of creative energy, and since we do this by choice, we are essentially limiting by choice any good we could obtain from it.

Spirit can only do for us what it can do through us.

By choosing to live your life relative to the Spiritual Energy Field of All Possibilities (Spirit and Law), you release the filters from being the source that determines what is possible for you. You are in effect consciously choosing Spirit and its values as your pure source of knowledge and power.

Adopt the perfect values of Spirit if you choose Spirit, and then watch the stars move in your life.

Speaking Your Words for Your Highest Good

Here is an example of how you can speak your words to co-create your life in the moment:

The Impact of Relative Filters on Your Words

I realize that I am one with pure Spirit. That peace, joy, and goodness is experience in every moment of my life.

I let go of every reference to past experiences and every reference to the collective unconsciousness of the human race as my source of comfort.

I only use my present condition as feedback on my journey toward life's rewards. Therefore, I always co-create the conditions and experiences that I want to have in my life.

Spirit is at the center of my being, as my life is being lived relative to the Spiritual Energy Field.

I know this is the complete truth about my life. This truth is now working for my highest good in every situation.

And so it is...

Discovering Your Star-Moving Power

– *Harold Davis once said:*
>*Your perception is important, because your condition is nothing more than an invitation that you have given to yourself, in order to experience it in your life.*

How you identify yourself in consciousness and what you relate to reflects who you want to Be. It makes all the difference and determines what you Have, what you Do, and how you move the stars in your life.

This chapter will assist you in discovering your star-moving power by answering two important questions: who you really are and what values you ought to practice in order to enjoy the positive benefits of spiritual energy.

Your gift of choice should facilitate this. Indeed, it's an easy task, provided you remain conscious of the choices that lie before you in mind and spirit and retain the will power to make your choice. If your will power is strong enough to opt for a life from the inside out, you will begin to co-create a successful, abundant, and joyous life. The starting point is your full realization that all the external conditions you sense through the five senses—taste, smell, sight, hearing, and touch—are illusions useful only as feedback about your human experiences.

External Conditions Are Illusions

Consider the statement: The external conditions you experience are illusion that you have created by your words, thoughts, and feelings. Upon closer examination, you will discover a truth that people ignore at their own peril. It says that what happens to a person is not what determines his or her future.

It is how you interpret what happens, and the choices you make as a result, that really count. This affects the quality of your health, your wealth, and the relationships you hold with others. Your choices help create a pathway by which you can break the patterns that manifest unwanted conditions from the words you speak, think, and feel.

Some Questions to Consider:

> *Do you often think about events that have caused you pain?*
>
> *Do you find yourself feeling like a victim of other people's prejudices and adopting other people's negative attitudes?*
>
> *Do you find yourself stuck and clueless as to why your life is the way it is?*

There is no reason why you should feel any of this. You have the ability to co-create your conditions by speaking your words. You have the power of individual choice and will retain it to the last breath, unless you surrender it to the unseen forces that can imperil your life.

There is a space between the stimulus of the outside world and your response to this stimulus. This space makes it possible for you to choose, not just pick from the medley selection of the past, the collective thoughts of the human race, or the appearances of conditions. Your ability to choose is what promises to bring you into alignment with the spiritual laws. These laws will enable you to Move the Stars or co-create your life in just the way you want it to appear.

Imagine what it would be like to be the Creative Factor, to co-create your life, instead of just responding to a life manifested by a set of options accepted by default.

Spiritual Laws of the Mind

To discover your star-moving power you must first have an understanding of some of the important Spiritual Laws that can work with your mental faculties. They are Universal Laws that enable your mental faculties to co-create your success, and happiness.

Spiritual Law of Pure Potentiality.
This is the Law that relates directly to the Spiritual Energy Field of All Possibilities (Spirit and Law). Its creative energy field is, by definition, infinite. The key to your success is to realize and tap into the unlimited potential of Spirit by identifying with it, speaking your words with conviction, and having faith.

Spiritual Law of Intention.
Another important Law, the Spiritual Law of Intention requires that you have a true intent to co-create what you want, a real desire to become the person you must Be to co-create it. It's not a question merely of having a hopeful attitude toward Spirit. This Law is about making a solid commitment to experience the desired results by speaking your own words,

and by releasing all words thoughts and feelings that are contrary to your intent.

Spiritual Law of Cause and Effect.
This is one of the most important Laws. If you speak the right words, you will manifest the right results. So much so that it would be impossible for you to speak lack and limitation while awaiting a manifestation of abundance.

Abundance will be manifested only when you speak words of abundance, just like the farmer who plants a row of carrot seeds. What does he expect to harvest in approximately eighty days? Carrots, of course! The day a farmer's carrot seeds produce watermelons will be the day on which something awry will have taken place in the Universe.

Spiritual Law of Giving and Receiving.
This is the Law that creates the flow of supply. If you help people get what they want, you will automatically receive what you want. To be successful in life you should focus on how you could render service (energy) unto others. Help other people achieve more in their lives and your life will be filled with abundance, joy, and supply. Whatever you want to experience in your life, you must first give it away. The more of it you give, the more you will receive. Giving starts the flow of creative energy in your life, and your focus thoughts create the mold.

Spiritual Law of Detachment.
This Law states that you ought to trust the Universe. If you adopt the right pattern, based on Universal Laws, then you will produce the right results. You should never be concerned about the actual production of the results. It would be like a farmer digging up the seeds he planted the day before to

check their progress. This would be counterproductive and demonstrate a serious lack of faith.

Spiritual Law of Averages.
According to this Law, any activity performed consistently enough will yield a result that develops into a pattern of predictable results. The operation of this Law is evident when we observe the collective consciousness of the human race. The variables will normally distillate down to about an eighty-twenty ratio.

You don't have to be susceptible to the effects of this Law. You can rise above it by making a choice in harmony with the Spiritual Energy Field of All Possibilities (Spirit and Law). The power to choose is within you. Average results are illusions. You must choose to live outside of the options of being a human being in order to rise above this Law.

Spiritual Law of Least Effort.
This Law describes your harmonious alignment with the Spiritual Energy Field of All Possibilities (Spirit and Law) according to Universal Laws. When you are so aligned, you leverage real power to yield results based on the lowest expenditure of personal energy. Real power is energy that never depletes itself, so it would be wise to get on the side of the Universe.

Applying these Spiritual Laws and others and being the Creative Factor in your life are the secret to your success. The key is to attract like-minded people by your vibration, people who are inspired to move the stars in their lives with their words. You should always empower your relationships with a view to obtaining results like perfect health, positive business growth, and prosperity. The people you attract will follow the good example you set in mind, body, and affairs.

Moving the Stars With Your Words
Harold Davis, Msc.D., Ph.D

The Pattern of Success

Success and failure develop from a pattern. A failure pattern will consistently produce negative results. The same principle holds true for a success pattern—it will yield positive results. Once you discover a pattern that has positive results, all you need to do is maintain the level of consciousness that gave rise to it. You can vary the amount of activity if you want to change the results.

The formula is simple. No correct activity, no correct results. Some correct activity, some correct results; a lot of correct activity, a lot of correct results.

This formula has correct activity as its only variable. It will also work if you substitute wrong activity as the variable; only, the results will be quite different—and wrong, of course.

There Are No New Options for Being Human

All human beings face the same set of options in the Universe. The principal reason for this is that the gift of life has already been given to us. We each were born into life with these options, which were set when human beings were first created. So there are no new possibilities or options available for being human. Who can change his cardiovascular system merely by thinking? Who can survive by thought in place of oxygen? Thinking will not change the movement of the stars.

We were born into these options. These Laws, Principles, and Options have always been available to human beings as possibilities or realizations. For example, the Law of Electricity was no less a reality when Jesus walked the earth than it is today. We're well into the age of information technology, yet we operate within the same basic framework that is known and unknown.

Being under the direct influence of this framework doesn't mean we are aware of every possibility at every moment. What I have in mind when I refer to a framework are the Universal Laws and Principles that govern our lives. We must be aware that we do not just think our thoughts. We think the collective thoughts of the human race as members of that collectivity. Some of these thoughts are a standard set of ideas that all people possess at some level, either consciously or unconsciously—though most ideas occur at an unconscious level.

Among the unconscious thoughts, I include those that keep your heart beating or control your digestive system, to name two.

Let me offer the example of a puzzle with which you may be familiar. Imagine a puzzle made up of nine dots configured in a three rows by three columns pattern or matrix. The rules for solving the puzzle are simple; you must connect all nine dots together using only four straight lines and you cannot lift the pen off the paper until all lines are drawn and all dots are connected. The solution seems simple at first, as simple as the things we encounter in everyday living.

This puzzle is really a metaphor for the options before us. The set of options we were born into may be likened to the rules I gave you for solving the puzzle of the nine dots. The options into which we are born cannot solve all the problems we encounter during the course of our lives—no more than the rules I have given for solving the puzzle. These rules offer many options but very limited possibilities for a solution.

If you can grasp this about your life, then shifting your perception of who you really are becomes a realistic possibility.

Once you come to this realization, examine your knowledge from three main perspectives:

Moving the Stars With Your Words
Harold Davis, Msc.D., Ph.D

> *What you know in your life right now.*
>
> *What you know that you don't know about your life right now; in other words, what you are sure you are ignorant of.*
>
> *What you don't know that you don't know about your life; that is, what you are unaware of in every sense.*

What You Know.
What we know is knowledge that is rooted both in experience and in things that we can see. This knowledge has brought us to where we are right now in life. It provides us with a standard set of options that we all have the ability to experience, because we were born into them. These options are the Laws by virtue of which we exist in the Universe.

For example, each of us has a basic way of processing information built into our brain. We were designed by our Creator (Spirit) from a prototype that offers us the potential of functioning in the Universe as co-creators. Our brains have essentially the same design and functionality. The same goes for our physical makeup and bodily functions. We breathe through the same process, circulate our blood through the same circulatory system, move our muscles in the same way, perceive through the same five senses connected to the brain. All this allows us to sense the physical Universe and our own physical bodies. Clearly, the functions of every human being are built from a master blueprint. The only differences lie in the uniqueness of our expressions — in a word, personality.

Our basic options, or Laws, are the same, and yet you and I are unique. These options exist in the Spiritual Energy Field of All Possibilities (Spirit and Law), which are Laws that hold constant no matter where we may be in the Universe. Unless there is a significant change in the spiritual energy field, these basic options (Laws) cannot but continue to produce what they are currently producing in our lives and in the Universe.

When you really think about it, this is very reassuring. Your ability to hear, see, feel, taste, and smell, not to mention every other function, depends on the permanent application of this pervasive power.

What You Know That You Don't Know.
What you know that you don't know serves as an opportunity to seek out knowledge from books, tapes, teachers, or direct from the Spiritual Energy Field of All Possibilities (Spirit and Law). This is information that you're aware of but cannot see it. It could help you Move the Stars by raising the level of your consciousness.

Seeking what you know that you don't know empowers you to ask questions that may trigger a paradigm shift in your life. The answers to these questions could contribute to the quality of your life.

What You Don't Know That You Don't Know.
What you don't know that you don't know is the knowledge that holds the most promise of a qualitative leap in your life. Once revealed, this knowledge can increase your level of consciousness many times over. It is knowledge of which you are unaware and which you can't see, yet it can alter your life in a remarkable way should you gain awareness of it. It is often revealed through intuition and the proper application of the imagination.

Deep meditation is a common way to access this spiritual energy field. However, the type of knowledge I am referring to must be discerned on a spiritual plane, where you have access to all knowledge, the omniscient nature of Spirit within you.

What Causes the Breakthroughs?

The enlightenment that will inspire your star-moving power toward its greatest breakthrough is what you don't know that you don't know. By examining what you don't know that you don't know, you can make a quantum leap in consciousness, a major paradigm shift.

Now, let's refer back to our nine-dot puzzle. As you recall, we concluded that the set of options or rules we were born into could not solve all the problems we encounter during the course of our lives; no more than the rules given for solving the nine-dot puzzle could offer many options but limited possibilities for a solution to the puzzle. The solution would be a higher level of consciousness or a new level of thinking. To solve the puzzle of the nine dots and to solve life's challenges, we must think out of the box, so to speak. The options or framework we been attempting to solve the puzzle from did not offer the possibilities of a solution although they offered plenty of options to try.

Living your life from the standpoint of "human being" offers many options for living but very few possibilities for true success. To live a good life, you must get out of the box called "human being" and into the box that represents who you really are. This is the solution to the puzzle we call life. You are a spiritual being who has human experiences. This is the truth that most people don't know that they don't know.

Once you recognize that what you don't know that you don't know is the consciousness that will Move the Stars in your life, you are ready to proceed with an inquiry into the truth about Life. This inquiry must start with what you already know about life.

What You Know About Life

You know that life is, because you are conscious that you exist. Remember that a dog doesn't know it's a dog; a goose flies south for the winter without a conscious knowledge of its true nature. You, on the other hand, know that you are part of what we call life. You also know that your physical environment is at least partly the product of the way you live and think about life.

This implies that your level of consciousness is rooted in your thoughts, the interpretation of which you have gained from some of your conditions, your past, and those collective opinions of the human race that you have come to accept. This level of consciousness is highly dynamic and unpredictable. Most likely it is causing you to be in disharmony with Spirit.

The purpose of your life is the full realization of your human and spiritual potential. I am not implying that you haven't already evolved in a positive direction in life. All I am saying is that it might still be an unconscious process. Very few people participate in the choosing of their life's purpose, mission, and goals. Most of us merely react to conditions, especially those that affect us in some adverse way. From birth we were taught how and what to think, feel, and do. Childhood is a critical time in character development. The good news is that whatever the experience, it can start you on a path to a good way of living. It's possible for you to experience a life that is virtually free of debilitating problems.

I am not trying to convince you that your life will be completely free of problems. My book is not intended to lull you into another illusion. Meeting the problems plaguing a large segment of the human race head on is an illusion.

As human beings, we are capable of giving meaning to our lives, but few of us are prepared to handle many of life's challenges. If you've lived most of your life in this way, it might be a good idea to appreciate the negative impact that not knowing what you don't know is likely having on the quality of your health, wealth, and happiness.

Change your perception of the Universe. Change how you currently respond to it (being in it). You will end up improving your capacity to Move the Stars in your life.

You Need a Different Level of Consciousness

To change how you're moving the stars in your life you need a different level of consciousness. The same level of consciousness cannot solve situations that are proper to a higher level of consciousness. To transcend these situations, you must live your life relative to a source of knowledge that is in complete harmony with the Universe, and with the knowledge that you are a spiritual being having human experiences.

The only worthy source of knowledge comes directly from Spirit and Law (the Spiritual Energy Field of All Possibilities). Spirit and Law are responsible for creation and the perfect order of all things manifested in the Universe. This is the truth about the Universe, and there is something within you that knows this. I call this ability to sense the absolute truth Intuition in Action.

Intuition in Action

Your intuition is a creative faculty that your mind senses in the form of a picture, sound, or feeling. The key to using intuition is to be willing to venture within yourself in order to see, listen, and feel how the absolute truth is revealed from within by way of harmony with Spirit. To Be in harmony with Spirit you must be aware of Spirit and its Values. You must identify unconditionally with these values. This is the discovery of your real self and its Star-Moving Powers.

Not Always Critical

It has not always been so critical for us to connect in this way. Our physical environment once was a place where it was important, above all, to be physically fit and strong. Men needed quick reflexes for the hunt; women had to be alert to changes, etc. Today we live in an environment that is in many respects far more dynamic. Our lives keep us mentally agile.

To deal effectively with this kind of environment, you cannot rely on age-old approaches to life. You must hone your skills and your ability to unify and harmonize with Spirit. This alone will allow the power to flow through you, around you, and from you in step with the level of harmony achieved. It will empower you to co-create the kind of life you want and deserve.

The Difference That Makes the Difference

Telling the difference between what Spirit Creates and what we co-created with Spirit is very important and easy to do. What Spirit creates lasts forever; although it is forever changing its form. What you co-create with Spirit has a limited span of existence.

Spirit has created our being and given us mental faculties by which to discern the truth about ourselves and the power of choice. This is the difference that makes the difference. This is what empowers us to be the Creative Factor.

We are the Creative Factor, even if most of us fail to co-create results that promise to manifest the life of our dreams. We have the power to co-create and live those dreams. As spiritual beings, we are capable of amazing things! As human beings, what we accomplish is mostly disappointing. Worse, we feel powerless to effect the changes we want or which are necessary to manifest our dream life.

This is not an enviable position for you to be in. It will only waste the potential growth of your consciousness.

Raise Your Consciousness and the Net Will Appear

While no one ought to ignore the adverse effects of the surrounding events, you can choose how you represent those events in your consciousness and respond to them. If you're afraid, know this: by raising your consciousness, the net will appear beneath you.

Follow this advice and you will be able to control your destiny. Reacting to the events in your life alone won't take you anywhere near that destiny. Respond rather than react. There are many more resources available to you to solve the issue in hand. You'll make far better choices that way.

This information will allow you to interpret your life anew. Watch how your interpretation affects what you believe about yourself.

What Is the Structure of Your Life?

In order to have a Personal Impact, you will need to examine the structure of your life—namely, the blueprint of its design. Our primary responsibility is co-creation, but we end up with rules that are not intentionally designed to follow Universal Laws.

Rules help society maintain a certain degree of order, but they are not always universal. Whatever their true origin, they interfere in how we relate to life. Yet our success in society in many ways depends on how well we learn the unnatural system that we interface with on an ongoing basis. This impacts everyone in our society. The majority of us need to purchase food, clothing, shelter, and other items necessary for basic survival. That pretty well sums up the current environment—our social system.

Ask Yourself

Here are five important questions to ask about your consciousness:

> *Do I find it a constant struggle to pay my bills every month?*
>
> *Do I see myself returning to the same dead-end street, not knowing how to change or master my life?*
>
> *Do I feel stressed out and short of time, money, and answers?*
>
> *Do I find myself wishing, hoping, and praying for change in my way of living?*
>
> *Do I find myself uncertain or concerned about my health?*

If your honest-to-God answers to these questions are not what you ought to expect, realize that your response—however honest—is more a result of your present consciousness than anything else in the world!

Moving the Stars With Your Words
Harold Davis, Msc.D., Ph.D

You have the power to co-create your life—by speaking your words.

Understanding and Seeing the Illusions

Each of us without exception experiences what I call the illusions of life, which lead us to believe that we are not spiritual beings.

That is the Great Illusion of Life, and its roots go a long way back.

To deal with it, you need to get a good look at yourself. Start from the beginning. You were once dependent on your parents, other people, and familiar circumstances for both support and social development. You were a young child trying to find your way in the Universe, and in the process have developed conscious and unconscious patterns.

If your childhood was anything like that of most people, your experiences were predominantly negative, spawning both negative and positive impressions inside you. You carry all the tendencies, likes and dislike, good and bad, of your past. Most importantly, you have interpreted events in your life. After all, that's what human beings do best: interpret their experiences. But we do it not only as physical but spiritual beings. We give meaning to our lives. In the end, this is exactly what creates success or failure patterns in our lives.

Interpreted experiences are nothing more than the relative filters we spend our time trying to read and figure out. They are what make our personalities unique. They live on in our personalities and impel us to behave in particular ways in the physical Universe. They form the patterns and unique internal thoughts we store inside our personal memory and that can become the chief causal factors in our lives.

These causal factors are illusions. They are illusions because they are not from first cause, but only the conditions that secondary causes have created. This is why the conditions we experience are illusions. They are created relative to secondary causes, a far cry from the conscious choices we are entitled to enjoy.

The first cause that results from a conscious choice to live relative to Spirit is the only right choice. Its foundation is Spirit, and it rests on Universal Laws. Secondary causation is an illusion that changes much like the blowing of the wind.

Let me illustrate this point.

Imagine a dark room completely void of light. Someone brings in a lit candle. What happens to the darkness? It can't possibly go anywhere, because darkness is not a thing in itself, just a condition. As a result, it has no power over the candle light. If the candle light is the first cause in this case, then the darkness must be the secondary cause, relative to the candle light. Otherwise, the darkness would have resisted the light — saying, "I am darkness and shall remain dark," as it were.

You know that it will never be so. Darkness will always vanish with the introduction of light. Remove the light, though, and the darkness will immediately fill the room. Even in its absence, candle light is a creative factor.

The Truth Will Set You Free

You are the Creative Factor in your life. To co-create what you really want, you must see the illusion in your life. You must be true to your purpose before you can live up to your potential.

It's easy to find excuses for the things that haven't worked out in your life. Nobody knows more than you how many goals fall in that category. But excuses won't help you fulfill your life's dream. You can lie to yourself all you want, never openly admitting it, but nothing will change in your life through self-delusion. Lying can be a serious obstacle to your success.

Here are three important questions you should ask yourself:

Do I regard the lies I tell myself as true lies?

Do I cover up my lies in order to feel better?

Do I keep my word to myself and to others?

If your answers indicate frequent lying, then ask yourself this:

Why do I lie to myself?

Set yourself free!
The time to start living your dream is now. You can have a vision of tomorrow and a mere memory of the past. Not only that, you will not get out of life alive, so why are you playing it so safe? You will witness private victories well before you do the public ones.

Private Victories Manifest Public Victories

Oftentimes, the public gets no more than a glimpse of a person's private success, as in the case of an award. Or, someone passes by a beautiful home with luxury cars in the driveway and thinks how lucky the people are who live in such a wonderful environment. That person has failed to realize that one has to contribute a lot of personal time and discipline to be able to accomplish this.

People are not always prepared to discipline themselves to accomplish their greatness. For example, an author must devote many hours to writing a book before it is published. This does not include editing and finding the right publisher (or promotional agent). All that the public sees is the finished product.

Discipline weighs ounces, regret tons. But discipline is always a private victory. If you refuse to allow a day to pass in your life without reading something inspirational, learning something new, or having a private victory, you deserve success.

From this chapter, I hope you have gained insights that will help reveal the star-moving power that you possess. You must know that you have this power, and that Spirit has given you the gift of using it for your benefit and that of others. This power is yours to use but not to hold on to. What is the sense of having a million dollars in a bank account and never getting to write a check? The money would do neither you nor anyone else much good.

In fact, approximately 80 percent of people fail to produce positive, predictable results in pursuit of their goals and dreams. You can choose to rise above the Law of Averages and start co-creating above-average results in your life, the kind of results that will move the stars in your life.

Speaking Your Words for Greater Understanding

Here is an example of how you can speak words that improve your understanding of Spiritual Laws:

> *I realize that I am one with pure spirit. That Spirit flows through everything I think, say, and do.*

My life is divinely guided to discover the right direction to take, and the true application of the Spiritual Laws of the Universe.

I understand that life is a mirror that reflects exactly what I am experiencing in my consciousness. I know this is the truth about my life.

And it is so...

Using Your Star-Moving Power

– Harold Davis once said:
  I'd rather attempt to do something positive and fail, than to do nothing and succeed.

In the previous chapters, you discovered how to use the star-moving power of Spirit, and that the amount of creative energy to achieve this is in direct proportion to your level of consciousness, depending on your focus and attention. You also learned how consciously to become the Creative Factor in your life, and that your level of consciousness is the most important factor determining how you move your stars.

In this chapter, you will learn about the three levels at which you experience life and the effect your level of consciousness can have in your life. You will also explore how the creative energy that flows through any thought you have about yourself reflects that thought in your experience. Invisibly, your words, thoughts, and feelings co-create your circumstances.

Being One With Spirit

The stronger your consciousness of being one with Spirit becomes, the greater the flow of creative energy through you. This is one of the reasons why you should never hold grudges or criticize others. The latter type of consciousness is disharmonious with the flow of creative energy, because it flows in a negative direction. You must keep your consciousness focused and be the Creative Factor in your life at all times. Otherwise, your life will appear like a random roll of the dice.

Spirit Created the Universe

We live in the Spiritual Energy Field of All Possibilities (Spirit and Law) that created the Universe. This energy field contains everything there is, including yourself. It is omnipotent, omniscient, and omnipresent, as you know by now. This means that it is all the power there is, all the knowledge there is, and it is everywhere present in the Universe.

You must get this clear in your consciousness to be able to use its power for a definite purpose. Through this spiritual energy field you have been given everything needed to create a healthy, abundant, and joyous life. The key to receiving this gift is to be conscious of the gift, believe in it, and accept it. It is done unto you insofar as you believe.

It is Possible to Have It All

It is possible for you to heal yourself, enjoy prosperity, and have empowering relationships through the gift of the spiritual energy field that is within you. The source of this power is not something you need to look for. It is a spirit already within you. It is the power we have all inherited from our Creator. People are spiritual beings endowed with human experiences; yet we co-create poor health and poverty in our lives because we buy into the collective unconsciousness of the human race.

During his long years of research, Dr. Carl Jung formulated a concept of mind he called the "collective consciousness." For a concrete example, you may recall the "Hundredth Monkey Phenomenon" and how the minds of the monkeys started sharing information after they had reached a critical mass in their consciousness. This is exactly the concept I am talking about here.

Levels of Manifesting

The Created Universe is manifested at three known levels of experience: Spirit, Mind, and Body. These are the Be, Do, and Have activities we participate in. We may Be as spirit, Do as mind, and Have as part of the manifestation of the body of the Universe. This is the truth about whom and what we really are.

Let's look at these three levels.

The body, which is the physical manifestation of who we are, does not have the ability to experience itself. Knowing nothing about itself, it needs a greater power to experience it.

The mind is the power by which the body is sensed. It exists at a higher level than the body. However, the mind cannot experience itself, either; nor can it create its own thoughts. It needs a yet higher power, a Thinker of Thoughts, and a Witness of the Thinker.

That third level of manifestation is what I have been referring to as the Spiritual Energy Field of All Possibilities (Spirit and Law). The Thinker of the Thought is where our creative power comes from on our particular level of consciousness at the time we think the thought. However, the Thinker is not without a witness. The Witness gives us awareness of the thinker and awareness of our level of consciousness.

Based on this knowledge, we know that the possible levels of our experience are:

> *Body, which allows us to be a part of the physical Universe.*
>
> *Mind, which allows us to sense the body and the physical Universe.*
>
> *Spirit, which is everywhere present and is all the knowledge and power there are.*

Spirit has two important components that it adds to these experiences:

> *The Thinker that provides the experience of conscious thought, body, and physical Universe.*
>
> *The Witness that provides the experience of awareness of being conscious of the thinker, thoughts, body, and physical Universe.*

This knowledge enlightens us to our personalities, which are the way we are being in the Universe and are co-created by our words, thoughts, and feelings. Remember: Words, thoughts, and feelings create our beliefs about life and, by doing so, can co-create what we want and desire.

We Experience Life Only in Consciousness

After studying these levels of experience and how they are produced, it should be apparent that the only place we can possibly experience life is in consciousness. We can't experience life in the body, because the body has no awareness of itself. We can't experience life in the mind, because the mind can't experience its own thoughts. We experience life only in consciousness, the source of all things in our lives and more.

Your mind creates your life by having your thoughts, and the body is the effect of your thoughts. Therefore, to be the Creative Factor for your health, wealth, and happiness you must study first cause, or consciousness, and how to use it to co-create what you really want. By doing so, you will move the stars in your life.

Consciousness Can Be Life Giving or Life Depleting

It is the lower levels of consciousness that create poor health and poverty. They do it by introducing a negative energy flow through the mind and body, which then causes them to go out of balance. The imbalance can cause disease, lack, and limitations. To co-create abundant health and wealth, or to correct an inordinate condition, you must raise your consciousness to a level efficient enough for the flow of creative energy to help you.

First, you need to know how to achieve this; second, beware of the level of consciousness required to have perfect health and well-being.

The Map of Consciousness

Dr. David R. Hawkins, MD, PhD, has pioneered the mapping of various levels of consciousness. In his great popular book, Power Vs Force (1995), he used a discipline refined by Dr. John

Moving the Stars With Your Words
Harold Davis, Msc.D., Ph.D

Diamond called Behavioral Kinesiology to develop a map of consciousness. He employed this map to determine the levels of consciousness and the relative energy produced at various levels with great accuracy.

Dr. Hawkins proved without a doubt that unconditional love is the energy level or level of consciousness required to heal all disease and to manifest well being in mind, body, and all our personal affairs. Through thousands of experiments, he was able to demonstrate that before our level of consciousness reached the level that he labeled as courage, at which time the person starts to accept the truth about himself. The energy flow in the person's mind and body is negative, and therefore Life Depleting.

The truth is that we are spiritual beings who have human experiences.

In all honesty, the use of creative energy to build a more perfect life has not been widely researched. However, enough studies have been conducted to prove without the shadow of a doubt that such a power at least exists.

We're certainly justified and condemned by the words we speak, our thoughts, and our feelings. This is why you should strive for the courage to lift your consciousness to a level of being that enables you to explore the truth about yourself.

How to Raise Your Level of Consciousness

Briefly, the way to do it is by being in perfect harmony with the Values of Spirit. What does this mean, and what do I mean by the Values of Spirit?

Values are a function of your words, thoughts, and feelings. Developing and using your ability to speak is central, because the only means by which good health and prosperity will come into existence is through the power of your words, thoughts, and feelings. In short, you speak them into existence. If your words align with the Values of Spirit, you are, in effect, vibrating at a conscious level that holds every promise to produce positive results by way of positive energy.

If there is no alignment, then the words, thoughts, and feelings you deploy will lead to a negative effect in your life. Words, thoughts, and feelings must be at an energy level capable of producing an attitude of empowerment.

This is the proper method to raise your level of consciousness. But don't take my word for it. As John Randolph Price, author and the founder of The Quartus Foundation, stated unequivocally, "Words spoken from a spiritual consciousness have the power to mold substance and co-create positive experiences." "Molding substances and co-creating positive experiences" is just another way of saying that they impart existence to things. They give rise to entities, whether on a mental (for example, mental well-being) or physical plane (physical well-being). That's precisely what positive signifies: the presence of a fact, thing, or entity that you and I can observe.

Many experts besides Price have come to recognize the truth of these ideas. In fact, it's hard to miss. The reverberations of the spoken word are observable and widespread in society. We see them everywhere.

You're not alone in your struggle. Other people face similar dilemmas as you, and the similarities span the ages. Central to all is how to achieve the proper level of consciousness. For people of every walk of life and every epoch, finding the right approach to a happy, fulfilling life is a question of consciousness. Once they discover this, they attain heights of success they had only dreamed about.

Occasionally, they get a calling to become teachers. These individuals are valuable, not because we must be submissive to everything they teach, but because they awaken us to a power that lies within each of us. Even the humblest among us go on to teach others—their children, work colleagues, community, nation, etc.

Learning to raise your consciousness from others is important, but there is another, more private dimension: meditation.

Meditation as a Technique

Meditation is a powerful technique that you can use to raise your consciousness. Countless studies and experiments have recorded its salutary effects on both mind and body. Thanks to them there is now a strong body of scientific evidence to prove its effectiveness. So how, you may ask, does meditation do what experts claim?

In the terms we've developed so far in this book, meditation allows us to connect to the Spiritual Energy Field of All Possibilities (Spirit and Law) and cast away the superfluous elements that clutter our consciousness. The lives of many people around the world today are negatively affected by their personal history, the collective unconsciousness of the human race, and their present conditions. These three factors influence what you can and will achieve in life.

We've spoken about them before, calling them the three relative filters. If you're unsure what exactly they signify in your life, refer back to chapter 4. Nevertheless, let me recapitulate their effects in a single phrase: the three relative filters regulate our attitudes at an Average Level.

When your attitude is average, it occupies a level that is unlikely to produce a positive consciousness for you simply because the average person has a predominately-negative consciousness. This will ensure that you receive what the masses receive in their lives; after all, this is what average means.

While being average may be acceptable in certain respects—for example, in health of body and mind that we deem so important—there is a negative side to averages and averageness in general. Anyone hoping to rise to a level of success corresponding to his or her health, career, or dreams ought to stay clear of being average.

There are numerous examples for this, and we will have a chance to discuss many of them later. Briefly, though, when you believe in or express a negative level of consciousness, you are effectively producing a negative energy flow in your mind and body that will hurt you in the end. Averageness may feel comfortable for a while, but instinctively we all somehow know what it brings in its wake. A person living by the Law of Averages will eventually suffer from poor health, lack, and limitation. These deficiencies describe exactly the workings of the Law of Averages. In the final analysis, this law entails more misery than comfort in our lives.

You can choose to rise above it, first, by being conscious of it, and then by choosing not to be subjected to it. You have a choice. Indeed, you can choose to rise above any condition whatsoever, and you can do it simply by becoming a more loving person who consciously practices unconditional love. I'm not using love as just another example. Love is central to an effective strategy of success—and more so if we're speaking of unconditional love, because love is the only real impulsion in the Universe.

I know as well as the next person that there are no guarantees in life, but if there ever was an automatic relationship between two good things in life, whatever they may be for you, unconditional love is one of them. Unconditional love will automatically produce a healing flow of energy in your mind, body, and your affairs.

Moving the Stars With Your Words
Harold Davis, Msc.D., Ph.D

So, where does meditation fit into all this, you may ask? Meditation is a way to clear yourself of erroneous thoughts, the ones that affect your mind, body, and experiences for the worse. It will clear the way for a consistent practice of unconditional love.

Now I'll give you an example, a professional one that eloquently confirms what I am talking about:

I once worked with a client, whom I will call Jerry. He had the unmistakable feeling we all get when lack and limitation begin to permeate our existence. After a single coaching session, I discovered that he was suffering from a low self-image. Jerry defined himself primarily as a human being — in the limited, compromising sense that all but discounted the possibility of moving the stars in his life. Every person has his own take on this issue, and he certainly had his. The net result for Jerry was that, subconsciously, he didn't think he was deserving of success. He felt this way out of some misguided sense of guilt about past mistakes.

Many of us let illusions lead us through life — never questioning, much less challenging them. Anyway, this was his illusion, and I knew of only one method to overcome his personal inertia: meditation. This was the key to his recovery. Meditation has the ability to clear the clutter from the mind and give way to more productive thoughts. I taught him how to meditate about important questions in a way that would allow him to see the truth about himself. He meditated on questions like "Who am I", "What is Spirit", and "What is my purpose in life."

Jerry had no trouble staying focused on all these questions, and he did it long enough to train his mind to be quiet. Meditation cleared the endless chatter that goes on in so many people's mind. Practice helped him discover that there is no such thing as time and space in mind. From that point, it was just a step away to finding answers, and not just any short-lived answers. He had a growing sense that his answers came from the Spiritual Energy Field of All Possibilities (Spirit and Law). What he lost in jealously guarded illusions he gained in inner serenity, because the answers to his inquiries revealed a truth about himself that raised his consciousness to a qualitatively higher level.

If your answers fail to do this, then they didn't originate in the source of sources, the Spiritual Energy Field of All Possibilities (Spirit and Law).

Once Jerry realized that he was "one with the Living Spirit," his self-image was literally transformed to a higher level and he started moving the stars in his life. He had been subject to beliefs that needlessly held his mind back. Changing his beliefs had transformed his life.

We Are Subject
Only to the Effects of Our Beliefs

You are not subjugated by the beliefs you wish you had but don't, or the beliefs of other people. Each of us is subjugated only by those beliefs we hold in our minds. Accordingly, "it is done unto us as we believe" — not as we wish, but as we believe! If you sense lack and limitation in your body or personal affairs, you know that negative thoughts are doing what they are supposed to do: producing negative results. Moreover, your level of consciousness is creating these thoughts.

If this is no longer the situation you want to be in, choose a different path! You can change your level of consciousness, and by doing so Move the Stars in your Life.

Moving the Stars With Your Words
Harold Davis, Msc.D., Ph.D

Clearing a Space in Your Mind

To clear your consciousness of unwanted beliefs, you must clear the "space" in your mind's eye. Clearing your mind is exactly what will enable you to "co-create" more precisely the experiences that you want. Do this and you will have taken a major step toward finding the consciousness and level that are capable of manifesting exactly what you desire in your life.

Clearing the space in your mind's eye is equivalent to a farmer clearing the soil of all the rocks and weeds that clutter the field. To accomplish it, mentally designate an area in your mind as the space from which you will co-create. That's the space where you tell yourself: I must remove all the weeds and rocks from my mental garden that are sure to curtail my next harvest. Only you, the farmer, can decide how much of that soil you want to prepare, and this ultimately will determine how much harvest you are likely to see. The more space you clear, the bigger the manifestation of the good you are cultivating in your mind.

At this stage of the game, you should ask yourself this simple question:
How tall does a tree grow?

Answer:
As tall as it can.

You are no different than a tree, and I don't mean this as an insult! You can become as tall and as good as you can be if you only make the attempt with the proper conviction. The better you are at it, the healthier and more capable you will be in the future of fighting off infestation and parasitical organisms, which feed on your weaknesses in an ever-descending spiral toward helpless passivity.

I admit we can draw only the roughest comparison between ourselves and trees, because trees have no power of choice. They can only grow; whereas you can choose whether to grow or not, and by how much. The power is inside you, so decide! There is absolutely no doubt in my mind that you have the power to choose. All you need to do is clear your mental garden. And I don't intend this in a superficial sense: you have the power to choose effectively.

Try it. Meditate on your relationship with Spirit. Quiet your conscious mind. Examine your perceptions of lack and limitation, as you carefully cultivate the mental soil, but do it with a view to leaving behind all your past references. When you are done clearing your mental garden, then and only then can you make a choice of what you want to keep or introduce into your mental space. Be careful to bring only the images of what you want into your mental garden. I don't want to sound flippant about it, but the task is really no harder than removing the weeds from your backyard and then planting the seeds of choice.

This is how we cultivate our minds. We have to do it with our present awareness, which allows us to be the Creative Factor.

By cultivating this special space, you will find it easier to mold your every thought according to how you wish your life to be. Envision your life, no matter how grandiose your vision might seem at first. When you do, you will have gone a long way to establishing what you consciously want from life. Then release the word-seeds into the fertile soil of your subconscious mind; sow your own words, thoughts, and feelings.

Just remember to keep your thoughts pure. You can do this by meditating on the truth about your unity with Spirit. Meditation is based on the Law of Detachment. Avail yourself of it; this law will help you to experience the kind of life you

Moving the Stars With Your Words
Harold Davis, Msc.D., Ph.D

want. The trick is to detach yourself, and detachment rests on faith. Think of the farmer and his mental state as he sows his seeds. He releases his best seeds into the soil, but he never goes back to dig up the seeds just to see if they've taken root. His faith tells him that if he continues to do his part, the Law of Cause and Effect will do its part. Rest assured that the Law of Cause and Effect will work for you and in a manner not much different from the farmer's: it dictates that your words shall take root and manifest the results you envision.

For some people, the harvest will be meager. There is no aberration in this; things are as they should be.

The reason I feel confident in saying this is that most people are limited in what they co-create primarily because of their own mental barriers. There are several mental barriers you should watch out for:

- *Your negative past*
- *Cultural mental programming*
- *Environmental mental programming and its pressures*
- *Childhood mental programming*
- *Other people's opinions*

The mental programming to which we are all exposed can pose a serious barrier to what we want to co-create in life. This is why it's so difficult to achieve our goals and dreams without first changing the way we think about life, the way we view it, and the way we feel about it.

You must raise your level of thinking in order to change your life and move the stars in it.

Changing Your Level of Thinking

By changing your level of thinking, you can realistically expect to produce a completely different consciousness than the one you've been relying on to this point and which seemed to lead to nowhere you want to go. You will succeed in this enterprise only when you fully appreciate the role of the Relative Filters.

In saying this, I'm not trying to slip something under your eyes—like a new set of beliefs you positively cannot live without. You determine what your beliefs are. Just make sure they don't hobble you in any way. You know best your situation. The wrong set of beliefs will impede your path to success, because it simply doesn't correspond to what you want. On the contrary, it lies at the center of your trouble, if any, and there is absolutely no alternative to removing it from your path.

The mental programming and Relative Filters we have accumulated in the course of our lives cause us to measure things based on acquired habits. For better or worse, though, this merely guarantees the same results—thanks to the Law of Cause and Effects. You will harvest only what you sow. To improve your results, you must have a higher level of consciousness than that which created the initial pattern.

To raise your consciousness to a higher level, you must represent concepts differently than in the way you are accustomed in your mind's eye. Do that and you will discover a completely different perspective in your mind, one that perhaps you've never before suspected was possible. This is a perspective that is free of lack, limitations, and your habitual way of thinking.

It's important that you clear a space in our mental garden (mind). That alone will free you to co-create your life's vision. Such a space will enable you to envision what you want to see happen instead of what you've merely been hoping for. This is the space in our mind's eye where all things are possible at the beck and call of your imagination and your words.

It is done unto us as we believe.

The process of imagining gives you the power to completely change your life, because it's your words and consciousness that co-create your life. Nothing else you have, suffered, or possess equals them. Only when you reach this stage of awareness can you act as the Creative Factor. As the Creative Factor, you do and act differently from what you have been accustomed to in the past.

Just watch the result—you'll be moving the stars in your life.

If you have goals, dreams, something that you really want to have or do, treasure your vision. Hold on to it. It's more precious than all the negative images now cluttering your mental garden! You will need it to produce a stronger vision in your mind's eye that can serve as the mold for what you want to experience in your life. Your subconscious mind will take care of the details after that, so long as you hold to the truth about yourself. Don't lie to yourself and your stars will move for you.

That's when it starts to get real exciting!

The best way I know to give you a taste of this is through an example. Let me tell you about John, another client I coached a few years ago. When I first met John, he was just an acquaintance. I remember his facial expressions at our first meeting. He had this great idea for a business he claimed he had once been dead set to develop. I didn't have to excite him to any new plans; he had already been there. His problem was that he wasn't completely convinced he'd be successful. Believe it or not, his family and friends were advising him to give up on his "harebrain idea" and seek "serious" employment. In their opinion, as well-intentioned as they may have been, he needed a secure job. That, by the way, invariably meant being "just over broke." Their reasoning was based on current statistics: nine of every ten businesses failed in the first few years.

John had a lot of respect for his family and friends. It was enough to discourage him about what kind of outcome awaited him should he opt to go into business for himself. My view of their advice was crystal clear, but I had to tread carefully. The road to hell, I knew, was paved with good intentions! But I also recognized that John's personal hell was not knowing what to do with his dream anymore. Despite his initial enthusiasm, his vision was growing fuzzy; it was no longer clear enough to inspire him to move forward. So, John had remained stuck until he finally gave in to the pressure. When I ran into him again, he was well on his way to losing every last ounce of excitement he had about his dream of starting his business.

John's dream was born of spirit, and yet he had reached a point where he didn't know who he really was. He kept identifying himself in the universe as a man of limitations—a limited human being unable to move the events in his life, much less the stars above him. Therefore, he let all the arguments his family had offered for his welfare to impose themselves upon him. By the time he decided to hire me as his coach, these arguments had acquired a logic all their own.

There was no quick fix to John's problem. A few years passed before he and I met again, this time at a networking event. That was where he decided to hire me as his success coach. I had the pleasure of helping him see the truth about himself and showing him how to be the Creative Factor in his life. He began to progress as soon as he identified himself as a spirit in the Spirit (spiritual being), and not just as a human being. He learned to adopt some of the values of Spirit and live his life from the inside out (real self-referring).

Before long, he and I noticed a significant difference in his reactions and behavior. His consciousness was clearly growing as a result of his new perceptions. This, in turn, was increasing the flow of creative energy through him, around him, and from him. When John spoke his words and convictions, releasing them into his mental garden—just like a farmer would sow seeds into the soil—his business vision began to blossom inside him. It was manifesting its true form. Soon, people and resources were showing up at his door.

In the end, John had chosen the right course of action. In less than two years, he had an established business that was earning more money in a month than most people earned in a year.

Look at the Big Picture!

Stand on the peak of the mountain top. Don't dwell in the valley. Success is already yours for the asking. Standing on the peak allows you to see the truth about the universe and about who you really are. That's where you can speak your words with conviction, authority, and faith, and where all of the illusions vanish without a trace.

Illusions will vanish. They're not things in themselves. We give them energy, and that energy eventually turns against us. Illusions are like darkness. That's how you must think of them. Deep inside, you know that the darkness has no power over light. It's the other way around: light has all the power. Bring a light into a darkened room and the darkness will vanish. In the presence of light, any other outcome is impossible. I want you to know that this is true spiritually, as well.

Your words, thoughts, and feelings are just like that light, and your illusions no more than darkness—the absence of light. Let your inner light shine through on any discordant condition and that condition will vanish like the darkness. If you don't have enough faith in Spirit and in yourself, you will give in to the pressure. Surrendering your most precious, most cherished goals and dreams to the opinions of others, however well-intentioned, will only delay their manifestation in your life.

Be the Creative Factor

Before you can become the Creative Factor in your life, you must first have a clear vision of what you want to co-create in your conscious mind. This vision must be fortified with conviction and purpose; otherwise it will lack power. Secondly, you must be willing to let go and let Spirit work through you; this will add faith to your actions. And lastly, you must monitor the process of manifestation using your intuition for any progress in your consciousness. This will give you an idea of the actions you ought to take next in the physical universe. Your inner senses will help you judge that progress.

What you see may appear as a picture, thought, or feeling. Whatever its form, just remember one thing: you must live your life from the inside out (real self-referring) before you can be successful as the Creative Factor in your life.

Success Formula

You are now ready to learn how to use the Success Formula to co-create anything you want to experience in life. Make sure you harmonize and unify with the source of all power, the

Moving the Stars With Your Words
Harold Davis, Msc.D., Ph.D

Spiritual Energy Field of All Possibilities (Spirit and Law). You are in complete harmony with this source once you consciously adopt the values of the spiritual energy field in which they operate. Some of the Values of Spirit are Unconditional Love, Creativity, Wisdom, Harmony, and Power, as you recall from an earlier discussion.

Here is how the formula works:

The Process:

1. *Clear a space in your mind to create form.*
2. *Align yourself with the Spiritual Energy Field.*
3. *Speak your words with conviction and faith.*
4. *Let go and let Spirit work through you.*
5. *Monitor the manifestation process using your intuition.*
6. *Finally, continue to take right action based on what your intuition is telling you, until what you want to experience materializes in your life.*

When you use this Success Formula to move the stars, there is no limit to what you can have and do, because Spirit is your silent partner.

Speaking Your Words to Move the Stars

Here is how you could express yourself to move the stars in your life:

> *I realize that I am a spirit in the Spirit. That Spirit is pure and whole.*
>
> *I am one with this perfect Whole, in perfect harmony with it.*

Peace, joy, and happiness surround me and flow through everything I think, say, and do.

There is a deep calmness at the center of my being, a perfect understanding of my relationship with Spirit.

My thought rests upon everything in peace and joy and in cheerful expectation of my good.

I am more conscious of the unconditional love of my Creator—all lack, all fear, all falsehood are vanishing from my consciousness.

As this Power flows through my being, every problem is released. My expectation of life guides me into complete joy, and happiness. The way is made clear before me and all is well with my soul.

And it is so...

Speaking Your Words to Move Your Stars

– Ralph Waldo Trine once said:
> Every thought you entertain is a force that goes out, and every thought comes back laden with its kind.

You now know that the Spiritual Energy Field of All Possibilities (Spirit and Law) is the source of your power to speak your life into existence in the manner you choose to experience it. This is the process by which you become the Creative Factor in your own life and in that of others. This chapter reveals the proven techniques that will enable you to speak your own words for a definite purpose. By following the steps and practicing the principles outlined, you will be able to live your life by design. Not by magic, not by concentration or by force of will, but by the Law of Mind in Action.

The Law of Mind in action is the automatic process which creates everything that is manifested in the physical universe. The key to your success as a co-creator is to become the Creative Factor by co-creating your life's experiences and conditions by choice. The way to accomplish this is by speaking your words.

Speaking Your Words

Speaking your words to move the stars in your life is a process by which you obtain anything you want. Since wanting implies purpose, I am referring to a process that has definite purpose at its core. You cannot take the words you speak lightly and expect to get worthwhile results. Words essentially create the mold or mental seed that serves as a pattern for the manifestation of what you want to experience in your life. The more specific you are when you speak your words, the clearer the image created in your mind's eye. Therefore, you must provide as much descriptive information as possible about what you want to manifest.

Building Belief in Mind

When you speak your words, you are effectively building a belief in your mind by the power of those words, upon which you intend to act regardless of whether or not the information is true or false, good or bad. The subconscious mind has no choice but to accept that belief. It has no power to reject it.

This is why you should always speak your words with precision. Your words build the belief upon which you want your mind to act. The idea is to make as little reference as you can to the condition you want to eliminate or change. If you follow this advice, the right condition or experience easily is manifested by the Law of Correspondence.

The main reason for this is that conditions are not things in themselves. Therefore, it serves no purpose to redress what is mere illusion. There is nothing to change except the belief. We experience life (conditions) only in consciousness, and for that very reason must raise our consciousness high enough to change any unwanted condition or to create a great experience in life.

"We are in the world, but not of it," goes the saying. This has profound implications for what we are attempting to do here. Your thoughts (words) are merely your personal projections onto the universe; your interpretations are nothing more than the conditions which your thoughts (words) have used for their co-creations. This doesn't make those conditions things in themselves. On the contrary, if the conditions disappear altogether, you are left with the possibility of realizing the purest visions. That's when you are closest to the Spirit.

This twin aspect of our nature—personal interpretations and co-creation of the universe within Spirit—gives meaning to our life. We accomplish our greatest feats solely by the power of the words we speak, along with our thoughts, and feelings, as long as we align ourselves with Spirit. Otherwise our accomplishments are random at best.

So, which of these two important elements of your nature is more important? You should strengthen both aspects, because they are both very important to the creative process. If you do this, you will not shortchange yourself.

What Is "Speaking Your Words"?

Whenever we speak, we formulate concepts that lie deep within us. But we don't just utter words mechanically. We strive to speak words with the conviction that they are true to our faith in the Spiritual Energy Field of All Possibilities (Spirit and Law), which accepts and translates them into some form or experience in our physical universe.

Beyond that, you will find only falsehood. Speaking the words of truth is the process by which we keep our thoughts

Moving the Stars With Your Words
Harold Davis, Msc.D., Ph.D

free of wrong beliefs and recognize the truth about the conditions and experiences we want to manifest or change. We do this as we see the Spirit with which we want to be in harmony. Whatever is true for Spirit is true for us. In this sense, the only difference between Spirit and us is a matter of degree only, not quality. After all, a drop of water is not the whole lake, but is of the same likeness and quality of the lake.

Speaking your word is an action occurring in your mind whose purpose is not only to correct a false or limiting belief but to transcend it. The only way that speaking your words can accomplish this is by planting new empowering beliefs that build images in your mind's eye. You think what you want to happen; therefore, you must refrain from thinking what you do not want to happen.

All contrary conditions manifested in the physical universe are only erroneous thoughts. For this you can count on the Law of Mind in Action. We know partly to correct this error in thought, but we must correct it at its source. The source of all thought is the thinker, and the only way for us to improve the quality of the thinker's thoughts is by raising our consciousness. When you find the thinker inside you, you find your real self: the Witness.

The Witness can choose to make adjusts to the quality of thoughts that the thinker thinks by simply aligning the thinker with the Spiritual Energy Field of All Possibilities (Spirit and Law), which is the real power that ultimately raises our consciousness. Your experience or condition will change only in accordance with the words, thoughts, and feelings you articulate through this unified expression of the Thinker and the Spirit. This union empowers you to be the Creative Factor and co-creator of what you want to experience.

Speaking about Yourself and Others

Real self-referring is the key, but when speaking self-referring words you should always talk about yourself, not to yourself. Refer to yourself in the first person. Say: My life, it's working for me, etc.

Speak your words to experience love, money, prosperity, wisdom, health, and to co-create or change any discordant condition. You can speak your words for any reason or thing you want, just as long as what you want will bring good into your life and the lives of others. You want your experiences to correspond to the Values of the Spirit.

If you speak your words for the benefit of someone else, you must speak their good in the third person. Say: Her life, it's working for her, etc.

The Five Steps of Speaking Your Words

You must implement five important steps when speaking your words for a definite purpose. Once you understand these steps and practice them in their proper order, you will experience consistent results whenever you speak your words. These steps will allow you to co-create what you want to do and have in your life. The results of speaking your words for yourself or someone else are never consistent independently of who you are. The key is to become the person you must Be.

The five steps of speaking your words in order of importance are: Recognize Spirit, Unify with Spirit, Realize the Truth, Give Thanks to Spirit, and Release Your Words to Subconscious Mind.

Moving the Stars With Your Words
Harold Davis, Msc.D., Ph.D

Step 1 — Recognize Spirit.

For this to happen, you must pronounce words in such a way as to visualize in our mind's eye the omnipotent, omniscient, and omnipresent nature of Spirit. You must know that there is but one Spirit and that we are part of its unity. Admit the recognizable Values of Spirit and acknowledge these values as your values.

Say words like: I know that Spirit created the Universe, I recognize that Spirit is all the knowledge and power there is, etc.

Step 2 — Unify with Spirit.

In the process of speaking your words, this step requires you to identify yourself as a complete part of the whole of Spirit and as having been created in the likeness of Spirit. While unequal to Spirit in quantity, you are both of one quality. Speak words like: Spirit and I are one, I am in perfect harmony with the living Spirit, etc.

Step 3 — Realize the Truth.

This is the most important step in the creative process. It allows you to be the Creative Factor. Spirit is always co-creating something for us, even what we inadvertently request at the subconscious level. Therefore, try to paint a picture in your mind's eye with your words and thoughts, which are the only knowledge that will represent what you want to experience in your life. Use words that embody the highest meaning for you. Remember, your utterance stands for a meaning that indicates the kind of response you should expect. By themselves, words have no power, but their meaning and the feelings they generate do.

With this step, you are speaking words that create feelings that connect you closer to being the person that you are, with the type of experiences that you desire to have. However, you must speak those words as if you already have what you most want to experience in life. It may not be true in a physical sense, but when spoken with conviction and faith your words will indicate that you have them—in a spiritual sense.

Speak words like: I have an abundance of money in my life right now; I'm healthy, wealthy, and wise; my business now produces great profits and I'm helping people live their dreams, etc.

I'm not suggesting for one moment that you daydream or fantasize ideas that are clearly frivolous. This is a creative process by which you co-create something in the Universe. There is a difference between belief in what you are in essence and what your passing circumstances are. How can passing circumstances measure up to the eternal? Standing still right at the point where the negative idea is introduced into your consciousness is the last thing you want to do if you want to rise above your lacks and limitations.

Step 4—Give thanks to Spirit.

Spirit is absolute; it has no reference to time or space. It answers your requests immediately in consciousness. So, use this step to thank Spirit for giving you what you've asked for, and then expect the physical manifestation to be delivered through the normal channels of the creative process.

Speak words like: Thank you, Spirit, for giving me abundance and joy, for the perfect relationship that you have blessed me with; I give thanks to you, mother, father, Spirit, for the manifestation of my perfect life, etc.

Step 5—Release your words to subconscious mind.

The fifth and final step in the process of speaking your words to move your stars releases the image you have created in your mind's eye into the mental soil of your subconscious mind. This is the same activity that a farmer would perform when he presses a carrot seed deep into the soil. Turn the word-seed over to the creative process of you subconscious mind; good will be manifested. There's faith in that.

Speak words like: I release these words into the flow of creative energy, I impress my words into pure Spirit knowing that they will not return to me empty of manifestation, etc.

The Process of Speaking Your Words

Speaking your words is a process governed by the Law of Mind in Action. Whatever condition you wish to reach or change exists merely as an image in your mind. It has no reality beyond that. It serves as a sign that everything is perfect and complete in your consciousness. The idea is to clear the Relative Filters in your way. This will unblock your higher consciousness, which is the only reality in the spiritual universe. You have to do this if you are to co-create the conditions or experiences you desire in your life. The way that you understand the truth is the only thing you should concern yourself with: the Spiritual Energy Field of All Possibilities (Spirit and Law), yourself, and others.

If you can do this—mentally embodying the truth in Spirit—you can bypass steps 1 and 2 of speaking your words and perhaps start speaking from step three. That's where you can say: I realize that I am one with the Living Spirit, or that Robert is a perfect child of Spirit, and then get right into step 3 of the procedure I've outlined here.

Demonstrate the Truth

Don't accept your ability to speak conditions and experiences into existence on blind faith alone. Demonstrate the truth. We should do this at all times, because results are the name of the game. Just follow the recommendations outlined in this chapter and give the technique and concept a fair test. There is no substitute for this. Do it in the knowledge that the truth will set you free—it'll allow you to discover the awesome power we all possess.

Difficulty in Demonstrating the Truth

Some of us might have difficulty in demonstrating the truth. You might need to stay with the process a little longer because you have been loaded down with years of negative conditioning and are unable to realize fully the underlying unity of life.

If this is the case, you are the one for whom you are speaking your words. You should speak your words specifically to release the effect that the relative filters are having on your consciousness. You are the person that is being affected, whatever the nature of your case. You should continue this process until the relative filter is dissolved and the truth is fully realized.

Use the Power

Remember that this power is for us to use, not to hoard. That's what I said before and I'll repeat it: a million dollars in a bank account is worthless if I don't write the check or use the money. By the same token, employing this power now is qualitatively different from keeping it for a later, undefined use. For it to happen, you need to have conviction, feeling, and be totally submerged in the realization of the omnipotence of Spirit. This is the power that will move the stars in your life.

Again, the best way to illustrate what I mean is by way of example. I worked with a client to develop confidence in his ability to manifest his goals, and dreams. I spoke these words for him:

> *I recognize that Spirit created the Universe. There is but a single power and this power is Spirit. It is the perfect and the complete presence of the omnipotence of Spirit that penetrates all things in the mental and physical universe.*
>
> *I know that I am only a part of this perfect and complete universe that is Spirit; however, I am in complete harmony with Spirit. Spirit flows through me, around me, and from me. Spirit is right where I am and I am in perfect unity with its omnipotence.*
>
> *I realize that Mark is a very important part of this omnipotent power. He is a spirit in the Spirit; he benefits from the flow of pure spiritual energy in every area of his life. His purpose in life is to receive the support of all the power and knowledge of Spirit.*
>
> *Mark's health, wealth, and happiness are now being manifested from the perfect consciousness within him. Mark's true goals and dreams are being fulfilled, because Spirit is right where he is.*
>
> *I give thanks for the infinite good and the complete fulfillment of Mark's dreams. I know that Spirit has given Mark all the gifts of life, and that Mark has accepted these gifts. He knows that these gifts are*

founded on the unconditional love of Spirit with all its wonderful values.

I hereby release the words that I speak for Mark to the Universal Mind of Spirit, and in doing so turn the entire responsibility for the manifestation over to the only creative power in the universe.

And so it is...

Perfect Health Consciousness

– Harold Davis once said:
> *Health is the real wealth. Lose it and you lose everything.*

It may be a cliché to say this, but health really is wealth. Until we lose it, most of us don't realize just how valuable it is. In this chapter, I will explain the Universal Laws and Principles that cause us to experience a more joyous, healthier life. You will discover how to co-create an abundance of health, vitality, and joy by the power of your words.

The Health Problem

Understanding the seriousness of a health problem is only the beginning. After that you want to be a part of the solution. To illustrate my point, I'd like you to imagine a well-known terrorist group that sends you the following message: "We are holding members of your family as hostages. If you don't meet our demands, you will never see some of them again."

What honestly would be your response to this message?

Same principle holds in ordinary life, even though the scenario might seem a little less farfetched when family members are dying or permanently losing their health. Would you share knowledge about the Universal Laws and Principles with others in order to preserve the lives and health of your loved ones? The best way to avoid a negative outcome is by using these Laws and Principles. They hold the only promise of perfect health and well-being. By applying them to your life, you too will experience perfect health and well-being.

Many people we know face the same situation. We have all been held hostage at one time or another, though the enemy might be very different. Every year, diseases kill over two million men and women in the United States alone. Each of us is at risk of dying or permanently losing his health. Yet the solution to this massive social problem is surprisingly simple. We're all part of an extended family called the human race. What better way is there to alleviate our health concerns than by sharing principles that make a real difference? What better way is there than to empower people to take control of their destiny by positively influencing their health?

Personal Impact for Perfect health

To experience perfect health you must use your Personal Impact. The impact I am referring to has to do mainly with your ability to see the illusion about your personal health. But how does this help you experience perfect health?

Using your Personal Impact allows you to see the true status of your health. Decide on the quality of health you want to experience, and allow you to choose the type of actions you believe will best bring about perfect health. But the very first step you should take, the one that will personally and positively impact your health, is to uncover the illusions of your health.

The Illusion of Health

Many personal beliefs about our health, including those we learn from various legitimate (and illegitimate) sources, are simply not true. We have been conditioned from birth to believe that only medical professionals can make the right decisions about our health. Some of us prefer to venture in the uncharted waters of marginal health-care ideas. All these beliefs can impact negatively on our lives. Although widely taken for the be-all-end-all of good health, they do not amount to sound living.

An excellent example is the fictional account of a film titled The Doctor. Actor William Hurt is a medical doctor who is insensitive to his patient's real needs—until, that is, he becomes a patient himself. Being a patient gives him firsthand knowledge of what lacked in the medical system. You don't need to be a doctor or patient to know what your true needs are as a person concerned about his health. It's in the public domain—in the sense that we all have essentially similar concerns about personal health, and we hold perceptions about the shortcomings of the health care available to us.

Here are two important questions you ought to ask yourself:

- *What part does the collective unconsciousness of the human race play in shaping my opinions about my health?*
- *What is the likely result from this level of consciousness?*

To evaluate your consciousness further, ask yourself these two additional questions:

- *Has my previous level of consciousness manifested the health I want and deserve to experience?*
- *Will my current level of consciousness give me the results I want to have now and in the future?*

Moving the Stars With Your Words
Harold Davis, Msc.D., Ph.D

After posing these questions, think deeply about your health situation. This will give you the feedback you need for an informed response. The results might just manifest the words, thoughts, feelings, or level of consciousness you most wanted to express, deep down.

Whatever you do, always follow the best mental pattern available to you in order to manifest the best possible results. This way, the results you engender will always be based on your current level of consciousness. You will be far more comfortable taking full responsibility for your own health than laying the blame on others, or delaying conscious action so that others might act on your behalf with their authorized treatments. Clearly, conventional treatments designed to deal with the effects of the root causes are not working. The best approach is to check the negative effects that impinge on our lives by addressing their true causes.

Briefly, the most common causes of our poor health are:

- *Our level of consciousness*
- *Our lifestyle and environment*
- *Our nutritional and mineral intake*
- *Our physical activities*

Spirit has created us with amazing perfection. We have the ability to heal our human bodies and maintain their energy without the help of chemistry or anything extraneous to them. This includes every imaginable drug or formula developed through medical research and the unparalleled technology we enjoy today. We have an almost religious belief in prescription drugs and other body-altering substances, whatever their harmful side effects; yet they will not do the job on their own. All we end up doing is to create an imbalance in the way our bodies function. It's too bad, because the illusion has adversely affected the quality of our health.

When you choose to have perfect health, you set yourself on the path to practicing the Universal Laws and Principles. This alone will have a Positive Impact on your health. Why? Remember that everything in the universe, including your health, is created on three levels: Spirit, Mind, and Body, in that order. Anything done at the mind and body level is either doing you good or doing you harm.

The Creative Process

The body is the servant of the mind. It obeys its patterns, and does so whether that pattern emanates from the conscious or the subconscious thoughts that operate automatically with the release of images into the subconscious mind.

Unhealthy thoughts induce the body to produce disease; healthy thoughts produce vitality, energy, and sound health. Our health is perfect when the words, thoughts, and feelings we speak do not restrict the flow of creative energy through the body. Speaking our words for good health causes the body to vibrate at a rate that attracts an equivalent amount of creative energy from the Spiritual Energy Field of All Possibilities (Spirit and Law).

You must always remember that disease and perfect health are a function of your consciousness. Look around you. Thinking fear, lack, anxiety, and limitation is continually destroying the lives of millions of people. Changing negative habits alone will not help anyone who refuses to change the words, thoughts, and feelings he speaks about health.

Let your words, thoughts, and feelings be whole—your negative habits will automatically change. This is the Creative Process, where Spirit plays essentially two critical roles. Spirit is the thinker and the witness to the thinker. I've pointed this out earlier. We have the inborn ability to tap into its spiritual energy field and allow its infinite power to work through us. Spirit does for you only what it can do through you. By adopting its Values, by unifying with it, you become the Creative Factor in your life and in this manner co-create abundant health, energy, and well-being.

Your Thinking

Your manner of thinking contributes grandly to your health. The only pieces left in the puzzle after this are your levels of nutritional intake and proper physical activities. These are nothing to scoff at. Their level will either sustain the life and energy coursing through your body or ebb its flow of Life and creative energy. Nevertheless, your thinking always determines the outcome by virtue of the choices you make. Thinking is coloring your consciousness right now, as you read this book.

Law of Averages

With the subject of statistical health data, which allow us to study social conditions, we revisit the important concept of averages from our new perspective. There is no doubt that the Law of Averages, a powerful Law that relies on statistical evidence, sheds important light on the leading causes of death and chronic diseases, which are invariably linked to the activities of the mind, diet, exercise, and lifestyle habits.

According to the World Health Organization, more than twelve million men and women die every year as a result of cardiovascular disease—in most countries, that's up to fifty percent of all deaths. This year, in America alone, over 1.5

million people will suffer a heart attack. A million of them will die, over 300,000 of them without warning of any health problems. None of these people will get a second chance to take better care of themselves. We spend over $60 billion every year on surgical procedures to correct the damage done by cardiovascular disease; well over $20 billion on prescription drugs for treatment.

And I haven't even mentioned any of the numerous other ailments that seem to plague us. The US Bureau of Statistics reported that over a half-million people die each year from all forms of cancer, a hundred fifty thousand from complications related to diabetes, forty thousand from liver disease.

You don't need to be a rocket scientist to see what's going on. The health situation is frankly out of control at every level: physical, mental, spiritual, and economic.

If you suffer from heart disease, cancer, high blood pressure, diabetes, Lupus, chronic fatigue, stress, poor circulation, shortness of breath, or just want to avoid these problems, there is still a way out. Understanding and practicing the Creative Process will bring astounding improvements to your health. My research clearly shows that most people prefer to solve their health problems through natural holistic approaches rather than prescription drugs or surgery.

This is not surprising. Chronic health problems are directly linked to lifestyle. How you speak your life into existence though the power of your words and consciousness has everything to do with your present condition. Whatever your genetic predisposition, you can solve your heath concerns by changing the words, thoughts, and feelings you express or harbor inside you. You can cause your Stars to Move concerning your health.

Rise above the Law of Averages. Be conscious of the patterns that embody the divine spiritual concepts of our mind, and body—there is no deliverance from poor health without them.

The Practice of Modern Medicine

This is not to say that modern medicine has not made great strides in helping us understand ourselves better. The technological advances of the past forty years have been nothing short of breathtaking. These advancements have helped save many lives in medical emergencies; however, they are not equally suited for preventive or corrective procedures. All I'm saying is that none of this can substitute for spiritual growth. There is a better way. Relying on technology and technique alone is insufficient; it translates into long-term negative consequences for the individual and for society as a whole. The proof is the medical crises that plague the world today.

You need to be aware of this situation. You must seek choices that harmonize with your spiritual nature. Only correct thinking, coupled with proper nutrition and activity, can yield the correct foundation for your perfect health. It's a self-perpetuating cycle—in an ascending as well as descending sense. The more you practice this holistic approach, the better your inspiration for positive thoughts, nutrition, exercise, and lifestyle, and the more spiritually, mentally, and physically fit you become.

In the end, the correct spiritual foundation that balances the correct mental pattern and physical support will provide the perfect health we all deserve to experience in life.

Health Is the Real Wealth

Most people fail to recognize the wealth in their health, until it's too late. It is in your best interest to implement the correct health patterns before your health condition reaches a critical point. I have spoken about health, the causes of its deterioration, and the solution on countless occasions — lectures, conferences, small groups. It all boils down to consciousness failing to produce the right pattern of behavior. In a word, we're not always aware of the truth about ourselves — it's what you don't know that you don't know.

This reminds me of the story about the mythical fish and its search for the magical water. Water is the most important thing to a fish's life, its lifeblood. Anyway, this fish had heard plenty of fish-lore, one of which led it to believe it could discover the mystery of mysteries about magical water. Lo and behold, this brave and adventurous fish began a journey to locate the missing central piece of its underwater puzzle. According to fish-lore, finding it was the key to life for all the creatures of the sea. So, it swam the seven seas; its whole life was dedicated to the search for this magical water. One day, it came across an irresistibly beautiful object. The appeal of this object, it was said, was so great that other fishes were wont to swallow what they saw of it without thinking.

Sure enough, our hero ended up hooked just like others before it. Our brave creature of the sea had mistaken the object for food. Unknown to it at the time, the object was a baited hook cast by a skilled fisherman. It was no contest. The fisherman was able to reel the fish in almost effortlessly, as he had done with so many other fish. Once out of the water and in the boat, the fish naturally noticed the change of environment, most notably its inability to breath. "Water, water! Put me back into the water," it exclaimed, but it was already beyond help.

The message of this story is that the fish discovered water last! Its long and hard journey through life in search of magical water turned out to be in vain. The magical water was all around it, but the fish did not realize it until it was too late.

Don't be like that fish, searching for what you already possess but don't know it. Don't discover your creative energy last. It is your lifeblood!

Health Consciousness

Perfect health is a direct result of our level of consciousness. Behind every cell and organ in the body there is a spiritual concept that is the source of its design. This is the omniscient nature of Spirit, which knows how to build everything in the universe, including a spiritual being with human experiences.

Each of us is built from the same spiritual concept that is the universal blueprint of every cell and organ in our body. There is a spiritual concept of the heart, brain, liver, eyes, etc. This spiritual concept could be compared to the architect who builds the DNA of every living thing in the universe. It gives us our unique appearance, but the basic function of our being is the same for everyone regardless of race, creed, or color. The same concept holds true for the limitless species of animals, plants, and insects, as well.

The spiritual idea or health consciousness inside of us creates the pattern of health. That pattern is the natural state for each of us regardless of appearance. It is the best reason why we need to maintain our health consciousness at the spiritual, mental, and physical levels. The only way to maintain health consciousness is by being a person who is real self-referring; in other words, one who lives life relative to the Spiritual Energy Field of All Possibilities (Spirit and Law).

Whenever we start living our life relative to personal history, collective consciousness, and present conditions, we introduce resistance to our level of health consciousness. This lowers the flow of creative energy through us, around us, and from us. Lower creative energy alters the vibration rate of every aspect of our mental and physical body. This is what determines if we have a negative disposition to the effects of germs, heart disease, cancer, ageing, and certain lifestyle factors, to name a few.

When our level of consciousness is incapable of supporting a certain spiritual idea relating to health, our pattern of health is subject to alteration by the Law of Mind in Action.

Because we are co-creators with Spirit in the Universe, we have the ability to choose the health pattern we want to experience. Whenever our level of consciousness is not life-giving, we easily fall victim to our own words, thoughts, and feelings. Our physical bodies and affairs are changeable. We have only to look to our level of consciousness for a solution.

Our body is subject only to those exterior influences that filter in through the subconscious mind. Given this, the only thing left is to choose words, thoughts, and feelings which we can then consciously impress upon our subconscious mind. The idea is to build a habitual pattern of health consciousness of our choice.

Habitual Patterns

Every time we consciously choose words, thoughts, and feelings, we act as the Creative Factors in our lives, thereby co-creating habitual thought patterns that become constant, steady features of our consciousness of health. It makes it so much easier to manifest healthy conditions when our minds and bodies are already infused with them. That is how you can Move the Stars in your life.

Quality of Our Words

The quality of our words, thoughts, and feelings are inseparable from our health. Nothing is more beneficial to our physical well being than to practice this simple principle to manifest perfect health. It is the very foundation of health; it helps us build an attitude that is firmly rooted in health consciousness.

As we saw, the workings of the Law of Averages are such that the average person is subject to poor health, lack, and limitation. By offering yourself the gift of the principles of healthy living, you rise above false limitations, and you are no longer subject to the Law of Averages.

You may choose to rise above a health condition, for example, by believing in and consciously practicing unconditional love. It will create a healing flow of creative energy through your body and affairs.

What Is Illness

Illness is symptomatic of an inadequate consciousness. The level of consciousness in question is the part that needs healing, but the only way to find healing is by raising your health consciousness to an efficient level. If your mind has created a condition of illness, it can undo its creation. Mind has power over the body. We are subject only to those beliefs we hold in our minds—"It is done unto us as we believe, not as we wish."

Whenever you experience illness, know that words, thoughts, and feeling are lowering your health consciousness, because perfect health is always present within you. If you don't want to experience illness, then you can choose to change the mental image built in your mind's eye.

Unconditional Love Is the Key

Unconditional love is the level of consciousness that produces a healing attitude of mind. Building this level of consciousness is the most beneficial thing you can possibly do.

Under this rubric, many things are possible:

- *You could speak your words and experience perfect health.*
- *You could speak your words and experience physical endurance and a great athletic performance.*
- *You could speak your words and cure the incurable.*

This is what unconditional love will enable you to experience in your life. However, three important steps must be taken within this consciousness before we can speak of a positive impact concerning our health:

1. *We must understand the illusion;*
2. *We must know what we want;*
3. *We must take the proper actions.*

One of the biggest illusions of our time is that human beings have only occasional spiritual experiences. This is blatantly wrong. The truth is that we are essentially spiritual beings capable of incredible feats. This truth will set you free to move your star with your words.

Coming to grips with the illusion will afford you an opportunity to decide what level of health you want to experience for yourself. Experiencing perfect health is a choice; you have the power to choose.

A Personal Example: Reversing High Blood Pressure

In 1988, I was shocked when my doctor diagnosed me with high blood pressure. I was shocked because I had just completed the Houston Marathon a week earlier with a time that was my personal best. My doctor prescribed a drug treatment and informed me that I would be taking prescription medication for the rest of my life. My health condition came as no surprise. My family has a history of high blood pressure and heart disease, so I followed my doctor's advice.

Soon after I began taking the medication, I experienced negative side effects, but my doctor urged me not to worry about them. He genuinely expected me to adjust to the medication.

In situations like this, one is easily overwhelmed. We feel powerless to change our conditions, especially before a medical authority that keeps assuring us there is nothing to fear from the medication we need to take.

I am certain you can identify this as an excellent example of living life from the outside in (object-referring) and how this could have a negative impact in a person's life.

Don't get me wrong. I have full respect for doctors and the difficult job they have of saving and improving the lives of the people they treat. But I remember thinking to myself: This is not going to be my reality. I refused to allow high blood pressure to be a permanent condition in my life.

Not only did I make a choice, but over the next three months I engaged myself in a process of speaking my words. I stopped taking the drug after losing the symptoms of the disease. Incredibly, numerous medical tests over the years have confirmed a dramatic reversal in my condition. The fact that I had a genetic predisposition for high blood pressure did not matter.

Although I sincerely believed this would happen, I cannot describe to you that moment when I recognized deep inside how correct my method was. I had triumphed over an enemy that threatened to take my life away from me, along with everything I held dear, had I not made a choice to experience perfect health through the power of my words. With faith and conviction, I had denied my high blood pressure as a permanent reality in my life. As a result, the condition vanished without a trace.

Health Consciousness Achieved

The truth is that I had risen above the Law of Averages — my health improved to a whole new level. Having aligned myself with pure Spirit, I soon realized that my health consciousness was at an all-time high. I had achieved perfect health in a vital part of my bodily functions, but my new consciousness reverberated in other physical respects as well. For example, I used to catch one to three common colds every year. After raising my health consciousness, I have not been afflicted by any type of ailment at all, not even a cold.

And they say there is no cure for the common cold!

By keeping my consciousness centered on the truth about conditions, and myself I experienced more of the truth about life as a whole than I thought possible. It was a triumph in every sense of the word. The power of choice allowed me to decide, through my consciousness, that health was what I wanted to experience.

Choose Health

Once we choose to experience perfect health, we must take the correct action to co-create it. Taking correct action is indispensable; it entails the precise pattern, which in turn, gives rise to perfect health—namely, higher health consciousness.

Such action must occur at the three levels I've delineated in this chapter: Spiritual, Mental, and Physical. All conditions, inclusively, are manifested in Spirit, Mind, and Body. Mind manifests good or bad health in the body through thoughts; Spirit is the thinker of these thoughts. We are neither our bodies nor our thoughts. We are the Thinker and the Witness of these thoughts. The more we become the Witness, the more we experience pure consciousness.

Physical Support

There are patterns we can consciously practice in the physical universe that will support our desire to experience perfect health. If we implement these patterns, our health will improve. It's as simple as that.

Practice a pattern of deep breathing, drinking plenty of clean water, eliminating toxins from your body, eating nutritiously, getting the proper amount of sleep, and doing regular physical exercise. This pattern will support you internally as you go about co-creating perfect health.

If you look at this pattern as a gift, then what you should be doing is giving yourself a gift every single day.

Your Physical Gifts

1. The Gift of Gaseous Elements
Take at least five deep breaths from your abdomen several times a day. The air you breathe is the cornerstone of life. Every second of every day, your body exchanges carbon dioxide for oxygen to keep each cell alive and functioning. A rich supply of the gaseous elements that comes from the air you breathe will help you experience optimum health.

It is important to know that gaseous elements make up approximately 78 percent of your physical body. The breakdown of these elements is Oxygen 65 percent, Hydrogen 10 percent, and Nitrogen 3 percent. These are essential gaseous elements of your body. The other 22 percent of the body is made from mineral elements, trace elements and other nutrients.

2. The Gift of Drinking Plenty of Water
Water is essential to everything your body does. In fact, it makes up more than 75 percent of your body weight! Our capacity for nutrients, blood flow, respiration, and elimination requires adequate consumption of pure drinking water. However, our bodies cannot store the water we need to sustain life, so we must replace it every day. I recommend drinking two to four liters each day depending on your body weight.

3. The Gift of Eliminating Toxins and Parasites
Cleaning your colon and eliminating parasites is one of the most beneficial things you can do to help your body run more efficiently. Digestion is an import cycle that requires lots of physical energy. By eliminating the toxic buildup in your system, a clean colon and a body free of parasites will increase your overall energy levels and improve your health. I

recommend that you take steps to clean your colon and eliminate parasites from your body.

4. The Gift of Eating Nutritiously

Food has a powerful impact on your body. It determines how you feel and how your body functions everyday. A balanced diet rich in whole foods, combined with quality nutritional supplements designed for your specific needs, will give you the energy you need daily. They will raise your disease-fighting strength and ensure a healthy future.

In my opinion, our daily diet should be made up of 100 to 300 grams of carbohydrates, 60 to 200 grams of proteins, and 40 to 120 grams of essential fats. Feel free to experiment and find your best combination based on your level of daily activity. If you are an athlete, you will need much more nutrition than the average person will because of your activity level. This is why I have suggested a wide range for these three categories of nutrients.

Since the soil that grows our food no longer contains a rich supply of mineral elements, it is difficult to receive efficient amounts of these elements from our diet alone. To compensate for this we must supplement our diet with these mineral elements, trace elements and nutrients. The mineral elements that are crucial are carbon, calcium, phosphorus, sulfur, sodium, chloride, and magnesium. Approximately 21 percent of the body is built from these elements. Trace elements and other nutrients (vitamins) make up approximately the other one percent of the body.

5. The Gift of Sleep

Sleep is the period of rest during which your body repairs itself and rejuvenates every organ. Conversely, sleep deprivation causes cellular damage by limiting the production of enzymes and hormones your body needs to preserve its cells from premature aging and to keep them healthy. Sleep also has a powerful impact on your emotional health; it eases stress and helps you maintain a balance life.

6. The Gift of Exercising for Life

Your body is designed to move, and exercise is a good way to ensure adequate activity. Exercise increases circulation and the oxygen flow, nutrients, and water to your cells. Your Lymphatic System has no pump of its own; it relies on physical activity to purge the body of its deadly toxins. This is important. There is four times as much lymph fluid in the body as blood. Regular exercise also triggers your brain to release health-giving hormones and enzymes, all of which lift your spirit as well as bolster your immune system.

You should develop a regular pattern of aerobic and anaerobic exercise. Aerobic exercise is the type of exercise used to improve oxygen consumption by the body. An example would be walking, running, or riding a bicycle. Anaerobic exercise is the type of exercise done for the most part without oxygen consumption by the body. An example of this activity would be weight lifting. I suggest that these two important forms of exercise be performed together as often as you can. An example of this activity would be walking a mile with five-pound hand weights. Here are the benefits of aerobic and anaerobic workouts.

They will:

- *Let your lungs function better*
- *Allow your blood to flow better through the body*
- *Tone your muscles and reduce body fat*
- *Keep your heart healthier*
- *Help eliminate toxins*

Most importantly, they'll make you feel better!

The Spiritual / Mental Support

You must let Spirit do for you what it can only do through you. Don't live your life tied down to your Personal History, the Collective Unconsciousness of the human race, or your Present Conditions.

Walk by Faith, not by Sight.

Walk as you were meant to do by living your life from the inside out (real self-referring), rather from the outside in (object-referring). This means living relative to the Spiritual Energy Field of All Possibilities (Spirit and Law).

You know this is the best possible choice!

If you make this choice, you should practice a daily spiritual pattern of meditation, unconditional love, forgiveness, gratitude, and acceptance. This pattern creates the health consciousness needed to experience perfect health. If you view this pattern as a gift, then what you should practice is giving yourself these spiritual gifts every single day.

Your Spiritual / Mental Gifts

1. The Gift of Meditation

Living your life relative to Spirit means, in essence, developing a relationship with Spirit by identifying with the Spiritual Energy Field of All Possibilities. Meditate daily and you'll feel the sense of health and well-being that results from your communion with Spirit.

2. The Gift of Unconditional Love
A free, generous, and unconditional exchange of love will attract meaningful lifelong relationships. These relationships will bring you joy in happy times, peace and strength in difficult times. They will create a mental atmosphere that continually heals your mind, body and affairs— without interruption.

3. The Gift of Forgiving
Forgiving others and asking for forgiveness are vital to your emotional health and well-being. They affect your ability to give and receive unconditional love. Forgiveness is not an act but an attitude. The sooner you begin cultivating your attitude of forgiveness, the quicker your level of anger, frustration or guilt will recede—to be replaced by peace, love and joy.

4. The Gift of Gratitude
Being grateful will lift you up and inspire you. So, appreciate everything you have in your life. Appreciation will allow you to harness the capacity to express joy and happiness in your life. Thankfulness is part of practically every culture; in America we celebrate it through a special holiday. If you're not doing it already, start celebrating the blessings in your life. Pronounce and feel your gratitude every day of your life.

5. The Gift of Acceptance
Develop your ability to identify and accept the circumstances in your life, without neglecting to strive for positive change whenever and wherever you can. You may have worked diligently to obtain or change something with success, and the only thing left is accepting the changes you spoke your words to accomplish. To ensure long-term success, always speak your words for the highest good of everyone that might be

implicated in the change. The fruit of this particular labor will be lasting peace of mind.

Speaking Your Words

Your words, thoughts, and feelings are the mental seeds (molds) that collectively serve as the blueprint for what you want to experience in your life. This is especially true for health. You can speak your perfect health into existence by building an image in your mind's eye that is in perfect harmony with the Spiritual Energy Field of All Possibilities (Spirit and Law). By adopting the Values associated with Spirit, by uniting your identity with these values—making them part of you—you will be well on your way to finding the right mold for what you want to achieve in life.

You are the co-creator, but it is Spirit that will bring things to pass for you. Therefore, your words, thoughts, and feelings may co-create your body's health conditions, but it is Spirit that creates your body out of itself. Your job is to provide the correct mental images for your Subconscious Mind, and to do it in perfect harmony with the Spiritual Energy Field of All Possibilities (Spirit and Law). It will give you access to the unrestricted flow of creative energy though, around, and from you.

That's how we nurture our bodies back to perfect balance, the perfection for which they were designed.

The Creative Factor for Health

The goal is to be the Creative Factor regarding your own health. To accomplish this you must, first, build yourself a vision of the kind of health you really want for yourself. Fortify your vision with conviction and purpose; these will endow it with immeasurable power. Secondly, you must be willing to let go and let Spirit work through you. None of this is possible without faith—so you need faith in every action you undertake. Lastly, monitor the process of manifestation using your intuition.

The end result should be an instinctive sense of progress that appears as a picture, thought, or feeling. This is what it means to live life from the inside out (real self-referring). It's the very definition of being the Creative Factor.

My Story

When I was twenty-one, I was an all-American track star, a two-year letterman at Texas A&M University. I had aspiration to earn a spot on the 1976 Olympic Team. I love Track & Field and I wanted to achieve my highest potential.

In the spring of 1974, my mother died after an accident. My father died exactly a year later; he was heartbroken and a perfect testament to the power of the mind. His love for my mother made it difficult for him to continue living after she passed on. They left behind two daughters and three sons. My youngest sister was under ten at the time, and there was no one willing to care for her so I made a selfless decision in the fall semester of 1975 to relinquish my track scholarship and career to care for my younger sister. To make a long story short, I walked away from a track career while in my prime and filled with unfulfilled aspirations.

For many years thereafter, I expressed my desire to compete in my favorite sport, and for the chance to reach my potential. I stayed active over the years, competing on occasions but never really testing my potential. The pressure of career and family dictated my priorities.

Moving the Stars With Your Words
Harold Davis, Msc.D., Ph.D

I am pleased to tell you that I am competing again. I am currently an All-American masters' athlete, with one of the fastest times in the world in the 400 meter run.

It hasn't been easy to achieve. It took me two years of mind and body discipline to be able to compete with myself and to work out at a level that would allow me to achieve world-class status again, relative to my age. I have finally reached this point in my return journey; my goal now is to achieve a time that equals the master's world record for category of fifty to fifty-four-year olds. While writing this book, I am running times athletes fifteen years my junior would have a hard time making.

When I look back to the private victories I'd had to achieve just to reach my current level of health consciousness, I consider this a star-moving experience in my life. It confirms much of what I have discussed in this book about our ability to move the stars, no matter what they may be.

The creative process has richly rewarded me in perfect health. It has reversed my aging process, as well as allowed me to fulfill a lifelong dream I had of training alongside of my son in Sacramento, California. Every time I think of it, I burst with joy at the privilege. I now have a son who has a passionate love for running, and to be able to teach him the pure joys of the sport has been exceptionally rewarding. He is now an accomplished runner and we enjoy our long runs together.

But although I was his teacher, he inspired me to continue through hard times, and there were many of them. I'll take private victories like these any time over public ones. Thank you again, son.

This story is being told for the purpose of inspiring everyone with a desire to reverse the aging process, to be more active in life, to lose weight, to quit an unhealthy habit, or to accomplish any health goal that requires choice and commitment. You have the power within you to achieve the same type of victories. All you must do is speak your word with conviction and faith—doubt will vanish without a trace.

Success Formula for Health

Once you have a grip on how to be the Creative Factor with respect to your health, you are ready to use the Success Formula to co-create a strong health consciousness that could translate into perfect health.

So far, you have harmonized and united yourself with the source of all power, the Spiritual Energy Field of All Possibilities (Spirit and Law). You're in complete harmony with this source and you have consciously adopted the values of its spiritual energy field: Unconditional Love, Creativity, Wisdom, Harmony, and Power—to mention but a few of the values you'll need.

Success is truly within your grasp. Let me outline the Success Formula in relation to health:

The Success Formula for your health:

1. *Clear a space in your mind to create from.*
2. *Align yourself with Spirit.*
3. *Speak your words for perfect health with conviction and faith.*
4. *Let go and let Spirit work through you to build your health consciousness.*
5. *Monitor the manifestation of your health goals using your intuition.*
6. *Continue to take right action based on what your intuition tells you, until you experience perfect health in your life.*

Moving the Stars With Your Words
Harold Davis, Msc.D., Ph.D

Use the Success Formula to build a strong health consciousness and there will be no limit to your good health. Your words will move your stars and you will experience perfect health.

Here are some words I spoke with success to help one of my clients develop a viable health consciousness:

> *I realize that Sharon is a very important part of the omnipotent power of the Universe. She is a spirit in the Spirit. She benefits from the abundant flow of spiritual energy in every aspect of her life. She has the perfect and complete support of all the power and knowledge of Spirit.*
>
> *All reference to her personal history, the collective unconsciousness, and present conditions are completely removed as a basis for her health consciousness.*
>
> *Sharon's health is now being manifested from the perfect consciousness that is within her. Sharon's health goals are being fulfilled, because Spirit is right where she is.*
>
> *I give thanks for the infinite good and the complete fulfillment of Sharon's dreams. I know that Spirit has given Sharon the gift of perfect health.*
>
> *I release these words for Sharon into the awesome power of the Universal Mind of Spirit, and in doing so; turn the whole responsibility for the manifestation over to the only creative power in the universe.*
>
> *And so it is...*

Prosperity Consciousness

– Napoleon Hill once said:
> *All achievement, all earned riches, Have their beginning in an idea.*

There are Universal Principles that govern the co-creation of successes and failures in your life. You should use these Principles to build a Prosperity Consciousness, which is paramount if you expect financial success. Once you learn how to use these principles to build a prosperity consciousness, you will be able to co-create the wealth you deserve to experience. In fact, you can draw abundance into your life with mathematical certainty.

Experiencing Prosperity

There are many ways to identify and experience prosperity in your life. You can build a fruitful relationship, profitable business, or a lifestyle that has just the earmarks of genuine, well-rounded prosperity. First, you must discover which Universal Principles to apply. Because we live in the Spiritual Energy Field of All Possibilities (Spirit and Law), which flows through everything including yourself, this knowledge lies within us. You must draw as near as you can to this power and unite with it.

Moving the Stars With Your Words
Harold Davis, Msc.D., Ph.D

What Is Money?

Believe it or not, money above all is a concept, not just coins and paper. It can stand for promise, problem, joy, solution, or sheer power. In short, money is whatever you want it to be. As human beings we attach meaning to it, so what it is depends on what you make of it. It is your definition, interpretation, and use of it that infuse money with reality.

With so many differing interpretations, it is a wonder that we can still use it with any common understanding. No one on the face of the earth will deny that we should have as much of it as we could use, because the physical universe we share dictates the use of money.

Fine, you say, but how do I create more of it? Before we broach this topic, let's examine some helpful concepts.

Money Is Energy

We use Money as a medium of exchange for goods, and services. In my opinion, energy is the best, most comprehensive way to describe and understand money. Most goods and services are the result of someone's effort, which implies the expenditure of energy. Therefore, it is useful to view money as an exchange of energy.

Money has no intrinsic value. Its value arises only upon the agreement (word) to effect an exchange. When you agree to exchange a portion of your time (energy) for a sum of money, you are exchanging your energy for a value you have placed on that money. When you exchange your money (stored energy or stored value) for goods or services, you exchange your energy for something you desire at that moment more than the money (stored energy).

Money Is an Extension

In this sense, money is an extension of the energy that flows through you, around you, and from you. It has no concrete personality that exists apart from you. Most importantly, it is neither good nor bad. Your thinking determines this. If you happen to live from the outside in (object-referring), you probably consider money to be very important for just about everything in your life.

If you are a person who lives life from the inside out (real self-referring), you are using money exactly according to what it is and not a whit more. To you, money is merely a medium of exchange for what you specifically want or need. You know that it is a flow of energy created first and foremost in your mind's eye.

Money Is Subject to Laws

The Universal Laws and Principles we have discussed in this book apply to money no less than they do to life. There is no shame in wanting to have money—far from it. However, there is one caveat: I believe that money makes us more of who we already are as human beings, whatever we may be. Anybody—employer and employee, buyer and seller, tyrant and victim—can own it. A lot of money merely helps its owner to become more of what he or she is, because money is essentially neutral with respect to each individual and to society.

Money Is Neutral

Why do I keep suggesting that money is neutral?

As energy, money doesn't give two hoots what it's used for or what it does for people, because it is not a thing in itself. It cannot decide anything of its own accord. Give a liar lots of money (energy) and what you'll end up with is a rich liar. Conversely, give a compassionate person the same sum and you have a rich compassionate person. If money (energy) is neither good nor bad, then no moral constraint can keep us from acquiring it. We are all, without exception, obligated to strive for it. The alternative to this is dependence on others for survival, and in the absence of a physical, mental, or age limitation, or some agreement for material support, there is simply no moral justification for shirking our duty to pull our own weight.

Therefore, we want to attract all the money (energy) we can get in life. In this, however, not everyone succeeds to his fullest potential. Only the person who is in perfect harmony with the Spiritual Energy Field of All Possibilities (Spirit and Law) is able to Move the Stars in his or her life. That person is certain to have a Personal Impact in the lives of many people as well as his own life.

Personal Impact for Prosperity

To enjoy prosperity in your life, you must have Personal Impact. Personal Impact is eloquent proof of your ability to see through all the illusions that cloud your Prosperity Consciousness.

Decide the level of prosperity you want to experience. Then, with the help of your intuitive powers, take the necessary steps that will lead you to manifest this prosperity.

Before your prosperity consciousness can manifest itself, though, you will have to discover the illusions on your own.

The Illusion of Prosperity

We hold many beliefs about prosperity which are simply untrue. They're mere illusions! We have them because the past and the collective unconsciousness have conditioned us to think in particular ways that are false.

For example, there is a misguided belief, which is surprisingly widespread, that only dishonest people are able to possess a lot of money. This is patently wrong. The same goes for the assumption that one cannot possess money and be spiritual at the same time. These notions have a negative impact on how we evaluate the information that directly relates to our prosperity consciousness.

Here are two important questions you should ask yourself:

- *What part does the collective consciousness of the human race play in forming my opinions about my prosperity consciousness?*
- *What prosperity is likely to result from this level of consciousness?*

Evaluate your prosperity consciousness by also asking the following:

- *Has my previous level of prosperity consciousness manifested abundance for me?*
- *Will my current level of prosperity consciousness give me the results that I want and deserve to experience?*

When you pose these questions, be careful to make an honest assessment of your current abundance. This should provide you with the feedback you need to offer a full and adequate response. The results will show up as a manifestation of your words, thoughts, and feelings; or to be more precise, your level of Prosperity Consciousness.

From this point on, you must seek the best mental pattern available to you in order to manifest the best possible results from the words, thoughts, and feelings you employ. These results will be based on your current prosperity consciousness. Take full responsibility for your prosperity.

Clearly, treating only the effect of the equation is not working in our society. The best approach is to address the root cause. That's the best way to avoid the negative effects that flow from it. The main cause of poverty consciousness is our level of thinking.

The Creative Process

Conditions are the servants of the mind. As servants they can only obey the patterns of the mind. They will follow the mind's patterns whether they originate from the conscious thoughts that you choose or the subconscious thoughts that operate automatically as your stored images.

Similarly, Poverty Thoughts cause lack and limitation, whereas Prosperity Thoughts cause an increase of energy. Prosperity is manifested because the words, thoughts, and feelings you speak do not restrict the flow of creative energy through your body and affairs. Your words cause the mind and body to vibrate at a rate that attracts an equivalent energy from the Spiritual Energy Field of All Possibility (Spirit and Law). Poverty and prosperity are a consequence of your specific level of consciousness.

Thoughts of fear, lack, and limitation are continually destroying the quality of life of many people around us. To change a negative habit or to start a new business—it doesn't matter what—will not help a person who has failed to change his words, thoughts, and feelings, or who has done it inappropriately. When you allow your words, thoughts, and feelings to be whole, your negative habits will automatically give way to positive habits, and your enterprise will be eminently successful. Words, thoughts, and feelings are made whole when we identify ourselves as spiritual beings. This is what you should do.

In this creative process, Spirit plays the twin role of thinker and witness to the thinker. Since it is the Spiritual Energy Field of All Possibilities, it creates the universe in its entirety. You have the ability to tap into this spiritual energy field and direct it to work through you. Remember, it can only do for you what it can through you. By adopting the Values of Spirit and by unifying with Spirit, you become the Creative Factor.

This is what allows you to co-create abundance and prosperity in your life by conscious choice.

Conditions

There should be no doubt in your mind about how thought can transform your experiences. It is time to let it work in your life. Money is a necessary component in every person's physical life. How can it not be? Money is energy. The services we provide for this energy is the other piece to the puzzle you should take heed of.

Your level of consciousness can either create an atmosphere that is conducive to the positive flow of money (energy) into our life, or it can work against that positive flow.

If you want to live out the rest of your life in abundance, you must cultivate a prosperity consciousness that provides the right energy for it. This will manifest the conditions that correspond with the specific vision you have for your life, and the vision will create the enterprise and the words you speak.

Attracting Abundance

Your desire—what you expect to experience—is the vision that regulates your Conditions. Your vision comprises the mental attitudes that make for an attractive power that may eventually cause the manifestation of the condition you desire to experience.

If a goal in which you have expressed interest fails to match your true desire and expectation, you will not accomplish this goal. Seeking something you do not expect to receive will not serve you in any way. You must believe you deserve it and otherwise have a reasonable expectation of receiving it. The mental attitude created by desire and expectation connects you directly to the Spiritual Energy Field of All Possibilities (Spirit and Law). This is why you should never expect a condition for which you have no desire. That's not too far from inviting the very condition you least desire into your life's experience. The more you do this, the more you fill your life with unwanted clutter. It is only a matter of time before your whole life begins to appear quite different from what you had originally envisioned it to be.

On the other hand, if you desire and expect an abundant and joyous life, it will come just as surely as the night follows the day. This is the Law of Mental Attraction in action.

Putting Energy to Proper Use

Money and the supply side of human activity are forms of energy. What you want and deserve to experience in your life is simply more of this energy. I realize that in making this assertion, I'm reducing complex processes to a principle, but this is necessary for a lucid understanding of what is going on beneath all these complexities. If you agree with the premise that money and supply are energy forms, then you are well on your way to formulating the strategies that will allow you to attract more of the same.

The first part of the formula is the simple recognition that energy is produced by the value of our words. A valuable word will be positive and active in its own right. What does this mean?

Just this, that a valuable word will trigger a positive movement in your mind that facilitates an exchange of energy. If this exchange is life-giving, it will generate even more value for all concerned; if the exchange is life-depleting, it will take away value. We add value whenever we use words to affirm the truth, but take away value whenever we use words to deny the truth. Words either attract money and supply or repel them.

Energy Flow

Put simply, energy flow is the flow of money and supply. Life's experiences offer every adult command of an unlimited amount of money and supply. The amount of flow depends entirely on the balancing energy of your words. Some of us are able to speak an abundance of words with attractive power. Others speak an abundance of words with resistive power: they tend to repel.

We can represent this principle in a single formula:

$A + R = E$

Where,

A = *Words with attractive power*
R = *Words with repelling or resistive power*
E = *Energy flow*

That is to say, Words with attractive power + Words with repelling power = Energy flow.

This formula should show you that the more words with attractive power you speak, the greater the abundance of money and supply that flows into your life. The lesson you ought to derive from this principle is that by increasing the attractive power of your words and eliminating their repelling or resistive power, you will produce a greater flow of abundance.

Fear and Consciousness

Fear is a level of consciousness that very adversely affects people's lives. It is probably the biggest reason why most people fail to realize prosperity. This is what most of us have to contend with as we work our way through life's many challenges.

Yet every fear is synonymous with false evidence, which often appears real. The best immunity against it is the practice of walking by faith and not by sight, as the master teacher once said. I understand how difficult it is for some of us to change a condition that we might be experiencing and to which we have grown accustomed. But conditions, always keep in mind, are not things in themselves. A condition is above all an experience we happen to be living within our consciousness. We use our five senses—sight, sound, taste, touch, and smell—to interpret our physical universe. However, the interpretations we concoct pass into our mind through our interpreter or mind-filter.

You are being object-referring when you do this, and only by being real self-referring can you become the Creative Factor. Real self-referring will afford you the power of choice for changing the condition exhibited—always with your consent. If the condition is overwhelmingly negative or pressing upon you, this can be difficult.

It is never easy to take a qualitative plunge. However, it never ceases to be a choice. Think of it this way: making a choice, no matter how difficult, is never as complicated as struggling to rectify a discordant condition.

We Are Greater Than the Fear

Fear can only be experienced in consciousness. There is no organ inside your body or repository of fears outside of it which can create fears. Our consciousness determines every fear we experience.

We are in the world but not of the world. Therefore, there is nothing outside of us that determines how we experience the world.

Another way of saying this is that we are all spiritual beings who nevertheless have self-limiting human experiences. Our five senses work closely with our imagination to create an experience we call fear, but fear lies only within our own consciousness.

Moving the Stars With Your Words
Harold Davis, Msc.D., Ph.D

The number of fears some of us possess is virtually endless. For people who are preconditioned to be fearful or possess an active imagination, this can be especially true. If you are that kind of person, then the thoughts entering your mind are tainted by a powerful emotion. Yet, it is nothing more than the fear of fear itself that you ought to be wary of. The key lies with your interpreter, or mind-filter. Adjust the filter and you will find yourself capable of handling anything you experience in your consciousness.

What you should do is to curb this developed tendency to seek security and freedom from fear at the expense of more important pursuits. Projecting your fear into the physical universe will gain you nothing of lasting value. Avoid it and you will immediately stop attracting evidence of fear into your experiences.

Law of Averages

Statistical findings give us insight into social trends and mass behavior. However, they are rooted in the Law of Averages. It is useful to keep referring to this law, because it sheds light on situations that hinder or impair our level of prosperity consciousness because we each have one vote on every issue as members of the human race.

For example, statistics show that over 38 million people live below the poverty level in the United States, perhaps the richest country in the world. The Median Family Income for a family of four is a mere $32,000 a year. Ninety-five percent of all citizens who reach the age of sixty-five do not have $500 in a checking or savings account to use as they please—this, after working forty to forty-five years.*

You or someone you know might be suffering from some form of lack or limitation, but it doesn't have to be this way. Understanding and practicing the Creative Process will lead to major improvements in your level of prosperity, lifestyle, and well-being. My research clearly indicates that most people—regardless of their ideas or intellectual inclinations—would prefer to live a prosperous lifestyle. If the major cause of poverty is the level of a person's prosperity consciousness, the logical thing to do is to speak prosperity into existence though the power of your words, thoughts, and feelings. By raising your prosperity consciousness, this will solve your prosperity concerns. Your experiences in life will rise above the Law of Averages, and your Stars will begin to move.

Dealing with Negative Conditions

A few years back, I experienced a major financial crisis that all but depleted my savings. But it wasn't just a personal loss. Over seventy-five associates had invested with me. You can imagine how I felt. To make a long story short, the investment I recommended to my associates turned out to be an elaborate investment scam. The truth finally came out after about a year of lies by our "investment administrator." It turned out that our money had been placed in a bank debenture scam. Our investment administrator had been aware of his error for over a year, but he thought up stories to delay us from taking action as he attempted to rectify his bad judgment, to no avail.

---

* *Source:* US Bureau of Census, US Bureau of Labor Statistics, and Social Security Administration.

Moving the Stars With Your Words
Harold Davis, Msc.D., Ph.D

My fellow investors were very angry. Some were so upset they blamed me for our misfortune.

In the end, the variation in their responses to this crisis proved to be a valuable education on the effects of money (energy) on people. The responses I observed depended on the person's individual relationship with money and, naturally, the level of their prosperity consciousness. What amazed me most was how little responsibility people were willing to accept for their decision to invest their money (energy). It was interesting that those who had lost as much money as I were able to adopt a better attitude than those who lost less. Many remained supportive and loving friends—in the midst of all this! We were all taken advantage of; our trust was violated. Nevertheless, I, along with those few friends, managed to use our faith to transcend this trying experience, in the knowledge that our investment was not our primary source of energy and that we lived in an abundant Universe.

Personally, by transcending the experience, I was able to reframe the experience into one that was far more powerful and inspiring than had seemed to me at first blush. I succeeded in creating a new vision for my life—by reinventing myself. I put together a five-year plan that allowed me to co-create the life I deserved and wanted to experience.

It was as simple and as enriching as that!

Some of the other members in our investment group continued to experience lack and limitation, which were due mainly to their particular interpretation of their financial condition. They were afflicted with fear and financial difficulties until, in the end, we were all able to transcend the experience.

This overwhelmingly negative experience had inspired the most life-changing period of my life. I can only speak for myself, but it gave me a period of focus that offered a chance to transform my self-perception and how I viewed the physical universe around me. I meditated to find answers to key questions in my life. Questions like "who am I," "what is my purpose in life," "how can I solve my situation," and "how can I be of service to others and to myself." My intuitive response was so profound that I had no doubt the answers I discovered were those I had been searching for most of my life.

My personal situation completely changed. I went from earning no money at all in 1998 to earning over seventy thousand dollars less than a year later. My income jumped to over a hundred and fifty thousand dollars the next year—and it is still growing.

In telling you this, I am not boasting about any business prowess I may or may not have. All I am saying is that it is possible to move the stars in your financial life by the power of your words.

Tough Conditions

During that period of perceived pressure, precipitated by the bad judgment and lack of integrity of our investment administrator, it was difficult to accord exclusive attention to the good things appearing in my life. However, at the height of the crisis, I was able to meditate, and this helped me change my experience.

Meditation, I have to tell you, had a preponderant influence on how I was able to change the sorry condition in which I had found myself in alongside the other investors. The collective consciousness, personal grievances, interpretations, and experiences of our investment group had produced very little by way of relief to the central problem we faced. Meditation allowed me to escape the physical limitations imposed by the situation. I now realize how much the practice of communion with the Spiritual Energy Field of All Possibilities (Spirit and Law) had allowed me to develop a relationship with my Real Self. But let me expand a little on this, as the path wasn't as straight or assured as you might think.

Meditation helped to change my daily condition. I soon found out, however, that while the conditions changed they did not go away. I was a stone's throw away from realizing something fundamental about my approach. The way I was speaking my words was not producing a permanent solution to my predicament. I had failed to use the Spiritual Energy Field of All Possibilities (Spirit and Law) — my basis for truth — to my full advantage. I was speaking my words relative only to present conditions. Sure, my words were moving each condition, but only into variations of the original form of that condition.

As soon as I discovered this, I began to speak my words with the purpose of changing my overall condition based on the truth, not based on the illusion of secondary causation. It literally transformed my experience into one that I could manage and change for the highest good of everyone involved. Furthermore, I was able to achieve this not only for myself, but also for other members of our investment group.

The Source of Supply

The Spiritual Energy Field of All Possibilities (Spirit and Law) is the source of our supply. Everything exists in it, and does so by definition, so everything comes from Spirit. Spiritual energy is the foundation of everything that you will ever experience. But while we all must have faith to benefit fully from Spirit, faith will not force or sway Spirit to provide directly our supply of energy. Faith simply allows us to cultivate our respective mental gardens, and to continue to plant the image we want in our mental garden or mind's eye. Beyond that, we harvest what we have sown.

When you understand this, you will know that you could never be poor or experience lack and limitation. You may not have money (energy) in your pocket, but this does not mean that money is not on its way. Prosperity consciousness may take you from a condition of having no money to one where money is plentiful.

Life is but an experience in consciousness. It will always be so, and we have only to own up to our role as co-creators who have the power to transform creative energy into whatever we want to experience.

No Competition

If you have faith, you can experience abundance in your life. This abundance bears no relation to competition, or what someone else has. Faith has everything to do with abundant supply (energy), and there is no competition over supply.

Where there is competition, there are rivals: other people who covet the same things you do. But your prosperity will never depend on what someone else owns. Supply (energy) is infinite, because creative energy is infinite. We've already discussed abundance as a spiritual value to which we can bear witness in the physical universe. Being infinite, the market on supply (energy) cannot be cornered by anyone.

You should never reason that if you fail to act fast enough on an opportunity you will miss your chance for prosperity. That merely wedges the opportunity between Spirit and yourself. This was the central cause of our investment group's failure to recognize the truth about the investment. Each of us has a direct connection to the Spiritual Energy Field of All

Possibilities (Spirit and Law); we cannot be denied the experience of abundance in our life as long as we keep our channels open to the possibilities.

Prosperity Consciousness

Your prosperity consciousness determines the amount of supply (energy) that flows in your life. If you are not experiencing an abundance of supply (energy), examine the level of your prosperity consciousness. We often ask Spirit to co-create something we really want to experience, but our level of prosperity consciousness is too low to allow it to happen.

We cannot experience more prosperity than what our level of prosperity consciousness permits. You can't go to the shoreline with a teaspoon and expect to carry away the whole ocean. You need a larger container. This is exactly what prosperity consciousness provides you with.

In order to experience more abundance in your life, you must raise the level of your prosperity consciousness. There are no two ways about this. Either your container is large enough for what you want to experience or it is not. If it is not, you need to increase your conscious capacity for prosperity, and the only way you can accomplish this is by opening up your heart and mind to the Spiritual Energy Field of All Possibilities (Spirit and Law). Do it and you'll meet with all the prosperity you deserve to experience.

Increasing Prosperity Consciousness

You cannot raise your prosperity consciousness without recognizing the presence of Spirit in your life. Spirit flows through you, around you, and from you. You have little to do in order to get into the practice of recognizing Spirit, since we all are completely submerged in the spiritual energy field. The more you recognize spiritual energy and turn away from the three relative filters, the higher your consciousness will rise.

The trick is to be consistent and persistent. Practicing the presence of Spirit is the most important activity you can undertake, and it is best experienced through meditation. Do your best to meditate at least twice a day—preferably in the morning before starting your regular schedule, when your mind is opening like the petals of a flower; and at night before bed, when your mind is ready to rejuvenate. This is what you ought to be doing to make a conscious connection with your source.

Keep your prosperity consciousness centered in Spirit every moment of your day and you will surely Move the Stars in your life.

The Creative Factor for Prosperity

To be the Creative Factor for your own prosperity, you must first build a vision of what abundance you want to experience. Furthermore, such a vision must be fortified with conviction and purpose to give it power. Secondly, you must be willing to let go and let Spirit work through you. This will add faith to your actions. And lastly, you must monitor the manifestation process, using your intuition to get a sense of your progress and of which action to take. This inner sense will show up as a picture, a thought, or a feeling.

You are living your life from the inside out (real self-referring) and you are the Creative Factor.

Success Formula for Prosperity

Once you are being the Creative Factor, you are ready to use the Success Formula to co-create a strong prosperity consciousness. Harmonize and unify with the source of all power, the Spiritual Energy Field of All Possibilities (Spirit and Law). After that, you must consciously adopt the values of this spiritual energy field: Unconditional Love, Creativity, Wisdom, Harmony, and Power—to mention only a few of these important values. Success is truly within your grasp.

Let me now outline the Success Formula, this time with respect to prosperity:

The Success Formula for your Prosperity:

1. *Clear a space in your mind to create from.*
2. *Align your self with Spirit.*
3. *Speak your words for prosperity with conviction and faith.*
4. *Let go and let Spirit work through you to build your prosperity consciousness.*
5. *Monitor the manifestation of your prosperity goals using your intuition.*
6. *Continue to take right action based on what your intuition tells you, until you experience prosperity in your life.*

When you use the Success Formula to build a strong prosperity consciousness, you will find no limit to the good you experience in your life. What you really want to experience is what your good is based on. It does not matter if the good you want is more money, more supply, more time, a new home, a new car, or better career.

You are now able to speak your words with conviction and faith, and manifest them into form as your chosen experience.

Here is an example of words I spoke with success to help one of my clients develop a prosperity consciousness:

> *I realize that Mike is a very important part of the universe. He is one with the living Spirit.*
>
> *Therefore, he benefits from the abundant flow of spiritual energy in every area of his life, because he lives his life relative to the Spiritual Energy Field of all Possibilities.*
>
> *Mike's prosperity is now being manifested from the perfect consciousness that is within him. His prosperity goals are being fulfilled, because Spirit is right where he is.*
>
> *I give thanks for the infinite good and the complete fulfillment of Mike's dreams, because I know that Spirit has given Mike the gifts of prosperity consciousness, and that prosperity is his birthright.*
>
> *I release these words that I speak for Mike to the awesome power of the Universal Mind of Spirit, and in doing so turn the whole responsibility for the manifestation over to the only creative power in the universe.*
>
> *And so it is...*

Empowering Relationships

– D.H. Lawrence once said:
> *I want relations, which are not purely personal, based on purely personal qualities; but relations based upon some unanimous accord in truth or belief, and a harmony of purpose, rather than of personality. I am weary of personality...Let us be easy and impersonal, not forever fingering over our own souls, and the souls of our acquaintances, but trying to create a new life, a new common life, a new complete tree of life from the roots that are within us.*

The quality of your relationships is a function of the quality of your communications both with yourself and with people, places, and things in the universe.

Just think: when you arrive at the end of life's journey, having lived through all the wondrous experiences you were capable of, you will look back and relish what you've done. The experiences that depict your life, every word, thought, and feeling you recall—all these will tell of your many relationships.

Relationships—by now you have learned how critical they are to your well-being. Relationships are far from a solitary experience. The life I am recommending is not one that you have lived to the fullest without many relationships. People should be part of your life; however, you should maintain control of your life. That is the only way you can be the Creative Factor in your life.

But what are relationships?

My definition of relationship is, simply, the condition or fact of being related, connected, or associated.

With a definition like this, however, one easily overlooks the fact that relationships are the most important aspect of our lives as people. We often forget that our ability to have rewarding relationships in various areas of life is what determines the quality of our life's experiences.

Empowering relationships give your life its harmonious, felicitous colors. Your capacity to raise their quality is one of the most important you will ever do as a co-creator. Your ability to co-create a happy life for yourself that you can share with others depends on it.

Remember, the level of consciousness that allows you to co-create such a life is the same one that makes you the Creative Factor, and it does it by allowing you to cultivate rich, rewarding, and fulfilling relationships that enable you and the people around you to Move the stars.

In order to build relationships, you must be able to connect. As Jeffery Combs—my friend and success coach—said in his wonderful book, More Heart Than Talent, "Open your heart, your energy, your charisma, because this is what people really buy and follow."

This is the kind of great advice that none of us can do without. I urge you to keep it in mind.

Relationships Are About Connecting

We all need to connect with people, places, things, and ourselves. Sometimes we're good in the one, but not the other. Try to do it in every aspect of your life.

Empowering Relationships

In the mental and physical universe, all people, places, and things are relatively connected. This is true whether or not you're conscious of the connections. We live in the Spiritual Energy Field of All Possibilities (Spirit and Law). Which begs the question, how am I relating to people, places, and things in my life? Now ask yourself this: What type of relationship do I have with myself? Because you must connect with yourself to become real self-referring and the Creative Factor in your life. It is important to your success that you maintain a great relationship (connection) with yourself.

Experiencing Empowering Relationships

Deep down, no one would deny wanting to experience empowering relationships. I'll go out on a limb and state further that the consequences of bad or dysfunctional relationships are nowhere more evident than in personal development. Dysfunctional relationships engender dysfunctional personal experiences, and more dysfunctional relationships.

Most of us have suffered them, and yet there is no compelling reason why dysfunction has to be a permanent feature of our lives. In the end, we choose to relate favorably to the people, places, and things around us; no one does it for us. Accordingly, healthy relationships can only co-create other healthy and empowering relationships. The Law of Cause and Effect demands it.

Our Basic Types of Relationships

In consciousness, we commonly experience four types of relationships: **animate beings (people, animals, and plants), places, things in general and, most importantly, with** ourselves. Endeavor to cultivate each of these areas in a way that enriches your life and the lives of others.

Your Relationship with People

Cultivating your relationship with people is very important to your happiness as well as the happiness of others, and it's not hard to see why. Many past experiences in your life have happened because of other people. But not all relationships are the same. Our relationships with people are of at least five important types: intimate, romantic, casual, business, and basic.

Intimate Relationships.
Intimacy in relationships suggests a connection that is both private and open. It's open every time two people open their hearts to each other; private when they share experiences, sentiments, or anything else to the exclusion of others. The latter type is characteristic of families, friends, married life or significant others, to name a few.

Romantic Relationships.
This type of relationships allows you to develop intimacy with someone beyond your family circle. The special, sincere attraction which occurs between men and women who connect in this way is based on the Law of Attraction.

Casual Relationships.
The people with whom you come into contact here may be around for a long time, or they may vanish from your life relatively quickly. Your relationship with them develops in the regular course of living, and neither time nor quality is a predominant factor.

Business Relationships.
Business relationships are the direct and indirect relationships you develop with people primarily for a value exchange (money or supply) measured in goods and services. They are often downplayed, even though their potential impact can reach people and communities around the world. In our global economy, it has become much easier and more secure to share energy through direct and indirect connections. Because of technological advancements and our ability to distribute goods through the Internet, global exchanges have become less personal. Superstores are a perfect example of this.

Basic Relationships.
You and I are part of a family called the human race. This means that, consciously or unconsciously, we relate naturally to everything else in the universe that is human. We share human experiences and connect through a single Mind. Basic relationships are equivalent to the Collective Consciousness, the bedrock consciousness expressible through what I have called the Law of Averages. We are each an individual part of the collective average, because every individual without exception gets to cast his or her vote, consciously or unconsciously, on every subject of concern to the human race. Unfortunately, most of these "votes" are hidden from view, whatever their impact on our lives.

From this perspective, the universe may at first seem cold and anonymous, but what you personally have is unique all the same and allows you to Move the Stars in your life.

Moving the Stars With Your Words
Harold Davis, Msc.D., Ph.D

Your Relationship with Animals, Plants, and Insects

We share a special relationship with the animal and plant kingdoms. For one thing, and we often forget this, we share space with them on this planet. We may adorn our lives with pets and plants, but we depend on animal and plant life forms as our main sources of food—not to mention the astonishing natural beauty with which they embrace us.

The earthly affinity we share with all these creatures is nothing to scoff at. The fact is that every animate being on earth has received the gift of life from the Spiritual Energy Field of All Possibilities (Spirit and Law), and each enriches the other, no matter which part of the natural order it happens to occupy. Even lowly, crawly insects play a vital role in this majestic balance.

Your Relationship to Places

Your relationship to a particular place, relative to everything else in the universe, helps determine how you experience life. Where you live—in other words, where you are at any given time in space—has important relevance to the events in your life and the rest of the universe.

What if you're in a place where you could save or influence the life of a man or woman without whom world peace would no longer be possible; or a person with an invention like the personal computer or the airplane?

The importance of each individual is relative to the other merely in degree.

Your Relationship with Things

How you relate to inanimate objects is no less important, and you must acknowledge it. For example, your relationship with the car, gun, or money you might own has an impact on the universe, whether you recognize it or not. This impact plays a determinate role in how life manifests itself at different levels.

Say, you've been acting irresponsibly with your car—like failing to stop at a red light because you were adjusting your car radio, or dangerously tailing the cars ahead of you at high speeds. An improper relationship with your car like this might have caused you to run into the side of another vehicle on the road. What if it took the life of a father and his child, thus starting a chain of events that altered the lives of the victims' family and yours? What if the event so negatively impacted on them that their path swerved away into long years of unspeakable hardship? Imagine all the tragedies that can befall so many people.

We are all connected. Countless other consequences flow from a single act of irresponsibility or caring that triggers a chain of events, even one we cannot observe.

Your Relationship to Yourself

Your relationship with yourself is by far the most important of the five basic relationships discussed in this book. The relationship controls the Creative Factor within you. If your relationship with yourself is real self-referring—that is, firmly rooted in the Spiritual Energy Field of All Possibilities (Spirit and Law)—then a direct impact on you and others is possible. However, if it is object-referring, it could be the cause of considerable chaos—rather than harmony—in how you relate to the rest of the universe. You may think that the repercussions of chaos are unintelligible for normal human comprehension, but they can be summarized into a single phrase: inability to fulfill one's life.

Chaos is the antithesis of a life of fulfillment and happiness. Its effects inevitably show up in the form of conflict with other people, places, and things. Wars are an excellent example of how collectively things might go wrong—even those wars fought in the name of peace or, worse, in the name of God. Paradoxically, it can also be a star-moving experience in the lives of people.

Having Empowering Relationships

To acquire empowering relationships, you must apply the Universal Laws and Principles we have been studying in this book to your mental patterns. Make these patterns a practice in your everyday life. This is the only way you will exercise Personal Impact, which you need in order to Move the Stars in your life.

Personal Impact

There are no empowering relationships without Personal Impact. Personal Impact is your ability to see the illusions in every type of relationship you encounter. Decide on the range and quality of relationships you want to experience in your life—and then make an intuitive choice of the action that holds the best promise of manifesting them.

To experience empowering relationships, however, you must first see the illusions.

The Illusions of Relationships

The illusions that accompany relationships result from the options we face and into which we are born as human beings. In an earlier chapter, I explained that there are no new options to being a human being. Let me clarify this.

I am not saying we have no alternative to being what we are, but only that all our human options are set and immutable. It will always be this way for human beings. The only way we experience new possibilities and choices is by being authentic and realizing our spiritual existence.

The biggest illusions we face is the claim that personality is our real self; that we are human beings with only occasional spiritual experiences; and that we are so irreversibly conditioned by our past and the collective unconsciousness of the human race that we are unconnected with everything else in the universe. Clinging to this belief is sure to leave a negative impact on your life—whether you consciously or unconsciously have the ability to evaluate the information about your current relationships.

As spiritual beings, we have an intimate relationship with each other. We are all brothers and sisters, because we all have the Spiritual Energy Field of All Possibilities (Spirit and Law) as our only creator.

When you recognize the illusions about yourself, you must opt for empowering relationships, and become real self-referring. The two are inseparable.

Deciding to Have Empowering Relationships

To have empowering relationships is to be the Creative Factor in your life. However, to be the Creative Factor in your life you must decide on the quality of relationship you want to experience, and adopt the values of Spirit accordingly. Without these values as your guide, you will remain subject to every swaying of the collective consciousness.

Here are two important questions you should ask yourself:

> *What part has the collective consciousness of the human race played in forming my opinions about my relationships?*
>
> *What quality of relationships is likely to result from this level of consciousness?*

Ask yourself two further questions to evaluate your consciousness of those relationships:

> *Have I consciously manifested the relationships that I want and deserve to experience?*
>
> *Will my current level of consciousness give me the results that I want to experience in my future relationships?*

While you are doing this, observe and evaluate your current relationships for proper feedback. The results will show up as the manifestation of your words, thoughts, and feelings — more precisely, the quality of your relationships.

Follow the best mental pattern available to you. This should allow you to manifest the best possible results through your words, thoughts, and feelings. Just don't leave your relationships up to chance, which implies lack of consciousness. The chief cause of dysfunctional, disempowering relationships is our low level of consciousness.

The Creative Process in Action

Everything that appears in life experience is the servant of the mind. Experiences obey the pattern of the mind and every condition created by it, whether that pattern emanates from the conscious thoughts you have chosen or the subconscious thoughts that operate automatically from images stored in your subconscious mind.

Dysfunctional relationships are a direct reflection of your level of consciousness. This is why thoughts of unhappiness, jealousy, and limitation can destroy the quality of your relationships. To exchange a known bad relationship for another will not solve personal dysfunctional relationship problems, if you fail to change your words, thoughts, and feelings about relationships. That is why so many marriages end in divorce. It is not the concept of marriage that is the cause of the breakup; it is the level of consciousness of the people involved.

When you let your words, thoughts, and feelings be whole, as they are supposed to be, your negative patterns will automatically change to positive patterns, and your relationships will then be empowered to change. Develop whole words, thoughts, and feelings simply by not living your life relative to the three relative perception filters, and by identifying yourself as a spiritual being.

Relationships Are Created on Three Levels

Like everything else in the universe, our relationships are created on three levels: the physical, the mental, and the spiritual.

Relationships do not happen only at the physical level, although that is how most people experience them. Thought atmosphere attracts people, places, and things into our life for us to experience. The thought atmosphere created by vibrations from our words, thoughts, and feelings are the mental level of the creative process that attract the people, places, and things we experience. The mental components of the creative process are critical to—though not the most important part of—establishing relationships.

The spiritual level is much higher than either the mental or the physical levels. There is a thinker and witness to thinking called consciousness. Consciousness is what determines the characteristics of the relationship. This is why higher levels of consciousness always create an empowering relationship, which has more creative energy flowing through it.

The Role of Spirit

Spirit plays a powerful role in attraction by providing the creative energy necessary for the creative act. Spirit is the Spiritual Energy Field of All Possibilities, the Creative Factor of the Universe. You have the inborn ability to tap into this spiritual energy field and direct it to work through you and for you. To achieve this you must adopt the Values of Spirit. This, in turn, allows you to unify with real power, be the creative factor, and attract an abundance of experiences and empowering relationships into your life—as you Move the Stars in it.

Relationships Are About Being

It is obvious from our discussion that the way we think is paramount in creating empowering relationships. It contributes most to the quality of our lives. However, being who we are in a relationship is the other important aspect of attracting empowering relationships.

Your thinking affects the consciousness you choose to live in. It determines the quality of interaction and the quantity of activity you choose to offer society and yourself. Your level of consciousness can create an atmosphere that attracts empowering relationships in every area of your life.

So, if you want to live your life with the type of relationships that empowers you, cultivate a consciousness that has a positive energy flow. This is the way to co-create empowering relationships. The Law of Correspondence, which governs this, can manifest relationships that closely correspond to the vision you want to experience.

Attracting Relationships

The quality of your relationships is a function of how well you communicate with yourself. Self-communication, along with desire and personal expectations, indicate the mental attitudes you need to use the power of attraction to manifest the relationships you desire to experience. However, your desire and expectation must remain constant, because they are fundamentally connected. Your main objective is to experience exactly the kind of relationship you desire, but you must believe that you deserve this quality of relationship.

It is as simple or as daunting as that, it depends on your level of consciousness.

One further point: You must consciously be able to articulate what you want through the power of your words. Your words, thoughts, and feelings are seeds planted in the fertile soil of your mental garden.

Moving the Stars With Your Words
Harold Davis, Msc.D., Ph.D

The precision of your words and the mental attitude created by your own desire and expectation connect you to the Spiritual Energy Field of All Possibilities (Spirit and Law). This is what creates an irresistible attraction field or vibration, which draws to you only the people, places, and things you want to make part of your experience.

Never seek a relationship you do not want to have; otherwise, you will be conjuring up the very relationship you least desire to experience. If you expect a rich, rewarding, and joyous relationship, it will come your way. This is how the Law of Mental Attraction operates.

The Creative Factor for Empowering Relationships

To be the Creative Factor in your relationships, you must, first, build a vision of what type of relationship you want to experience. Fortify this vision with conviction and purpose. This will augment its power. Secondly, let go and let Spirit work through you. This will add faith to any actions you undertake. Lastly, use your intuition to get a sense not only of your progress, but also of the actions you should be taking. This inner sense will bring forth a picture, thought, or feeling. Whatever it may be, just remember this: you must live your life from the inside out (real self-referring) before you can be the Creative Factor.

Decide to experience the relationships you, and only you, want.

Success Formula for Empowering Your Relationships

Having mastered how to be the Creative Factor, you are ready to use the Success Formula to co-create empowering relationships in every area of your life. This stage is exhilarating. I do not need to tell you that people and your relationships with them can exert enormous joy in your life. Now you are in command. Your life is not being swayed in this or that direction by forces beyond your control.

You have incredible momentum, but you must keep it up. Harmonize or unify yourself with the source of all power, the Spiritual Energy Field of All Possibilities (Spirit and Law). When you are in complete harmony with this ultimate source of power, you will be able to consciously adopt its values: Unconditional love, Wisdom, Harmony, and Joy, among others.

To Summarize the Formula:

Speak your words with conviction and faith. This is how you will start attracting empowering relationships. Let go and let Spirit work through you—it will raise your consciousness and allow you to attract the relationships you want. Then, monitor your relationships as they are manifested, using your intuition as a guide for further action. Continue to take action based on your intuition until the relationships that you want, have, and deserve are experienced.

Using the Success Formula to establish a strong and positive consciousness will attract unique relationships. The words, thoughts, and feelings you express within your own consciousness determine the quality of those relationships—

Moving the Stars With Your Words
Harold Davis, Msc.D., Ph.D

whether you intended all along to attract more friends, a lover, business contacts, or just material wealth. To speak your relationships into existence, acquire the capacity to Move the Stars in your life.

If love is truly your goal, let me end with some words that have worked well in assisting one of my clients in her desire to experience and maintain empowering relationships:

> *I realize how important Mary's Life is to Spirit. She is in perfect harmony with Spirit, and benefits from the abundant flow of spiritual energy in every area of her life. She lives her life relative to Spirit. Her choices are attracting empowering relationships into her life that fulfill her deepest desires.*
>
> *As I give thanks for the infinite good and the complete fulfillment of Mary's desire to have mutually empowering relationships, I know that Spirit has given her the gifts of unconditional Love.*
>
> *I release these words for Mary to the Universal Mind of Spirit, in all its awesome power, and in doing so turn the responsibility for the manifestation of her good over to the only creative power in the universe.*
>
> *And so it is...*

Moving the Stars in Your Life

– Helen Keller once said:
Life is but a daring adventure or it is nothing at all.

In this chapter, I will bring together the main ideas of this philosophy into a comprehensive view. We have discussed each concept in detail. Now I want you to picture this philosophy as if you were standing on the mountain peak with a commanding view of the valley of experience.

This overview should reinforce your insight into the primary objective: learning to be the Creative Factor in your life and to manifest what you really want. You will be able to experience everything you want to, which is the most important criteria of this philosophy.

Designing Your Life

Designing your life requires you to focus your words, thoughts, and feelings on what you really want to experience in your life. Nothing short of this will allow you to create a life by design. Focusing will spare you much wasted effort to avoid the pains and disappointments that result from an undisciplined life. Such an effort often leads people to give up on their goals and dreams.

It is a hard pill to swallow, but this is how things work for more than eighty percent of the population, and it is not hard to see why. If focus or the lack of it determines to what degree

Moving the Stars With Your Words
Harold Davis, Msc.D., Ph.D

we will live a life by design, then you cannot expect to experience what you want and deserve without it. Haphazard thinking without clear purpose will never get you what you want. You will not succeed without the right action plan. Even if you are experiencing new riches, or perfect health, you will never be able to profit from them in exactly the way you deserve without the right focus. You will not feel fully satisfied, because your life is not serving you. It is serving something or someone else, to whom you have relinquished your life. Just letting your life happen amounts to giving up on the way life was really meant to be experienced.

Why do I describe this as giving up on life? After all, most of us have sincere intentions and desires, and we work hard for what we earn, even if we have not attempted to design our lives.

This is not enough to make up for the lack of faith in our life. Faith is the basic ingredient we need to establish our mind's degree of focus. Belief cements all the varied things that may be happening in our life into a single focus. This is what constructive beliefs do with the proper faith. Central to every constructive belief is its ability to empower you to become the Creative Factor. If you want a life that is a daring and adventurous, one that leaves you glad to be alive and certain that you are a beacon of light to others, you must believe that you are the only Creative Factor in your life — a servant to no one and nothing else.

Like everything else in our world, there are many kinds of beliefs. Some of them propel you forward, others hinder you. You are the one who chooses which ones to adopt. Your choice will have a direct impact on the kind of life you will end up with. So, gather up your mental faculties and use your intuition; there is nothing to fear from what you, and only you, want out of life. Just as long as you are not paralyzed by the negative impact: limiting beliefs can contribute to your life.

Limiting Beliefs

Recall the limiting beliefs you had as a child. It isn't always easy or even pleasant, I realize that. Nevertheless, analyzing those beliefs might shed light on how they developed and what effect they presently are having in your life. You will learn how they have prevented you from achieving your highest potential. Your failure in this important respect is probably due to the image that those beliefs have created in your mind's eye.

Most people never stay helpless for long. They do things to change what they think is not working for them, such as beliefs. You have likely tried to modify or replace some of your beliefs. If those beliefs were no longer working in your best interest, that was a wise thing to do.

I would like you to renew this practice—if you've never before questioned dubious beliefs, this might be a good time to start. Ask yourself this powerful question:

> *What limiting beliefs do I have that hold me back from experiencing my life to the fullest, the way I want to experience it?*

The answer you provide is certain to reveal the limiting effect of those beliefs, which have done nothing but prevent you from moving the stars in your life. Since a belief is based on nothing more than a feeling of certainty about something, you have the ability to challenge it.

A Fire Walk Experience

I first learned about my ability to challenge well-entrenched beliefs back in 1992, although the fire walk that had triggered

Moving the Stars With Your Words
Harold Davis, Msc.D., Ph.D

this action was far from my last. There is no obvious social benefit to walking barefoot over hot coals—which by the way usually hover around sixteen hundred degrees Fahrenheit. I can only speak from my own experience, but I was able somehow to live an experience that showed me at least its metaphorical value. Let me explain.

Walking on hot coals for the first time challenged certain beliefs I had which seemed practically second nature to me. I want to avoid generalizing about all beliefs. My point has to do exclusively with those beliefs that have limited me mentally and physically. Feel free to read your own story into this, as long as you remember the fundamentals.

Before ever attempting the fire walk, I used to believe it was impossible for a person to prance safely over hot coals without burning the soles of his feet. Then, I discovered it was possible—and performed that feat without any smoke-and-mirror tricks. It was a revelation, yet I still do not know how I did it—not in a physical sense.

The reason I say this is that all I needed was to be convinced of the physical possibility. Yet, the idea started me on a spiritual journey that empowered me to take a good hard look at other limiting beliefs I had. To my astonishment, there were many I had never thought of challenging, let alone replacing.

Beliefs as Maps for Your Life

Beliefs may be interpreted as perceptions, a part of the map of your Life. It is helpful to assume that this map is not necessarily accurate, that it is no more or less than how you interpret the physical universe from a particular vantage point. In the end, it is you who decide. If you want a new experience and different results, you need only change that part of the map which impedes your path.

Map of Life

The map of your life represents the sensory-based information you sense from the physical universe, plus the interpretation you have of it in your mind. To modify any part of this map, you need to change your views. The highest view of life of which we are capable is the one that allows us to live life in complete harmony with Spirit.

The quality of what you experience, your mental images, and the level of your consciousness are altered by this knowledge.

Why We Suffer

I often wonder why so many people fail to live their lives on their own terms. Even in a rich country like America, which has so many opportunities to acquire wealth, ninety-five percent of people are financially challenged once they reach retirement age. They depend on the government, family, and friends to live at a basic level.

The explanation for this, as you will know by now, is that perceptions prevent us from living life at a level that reflects our true ideal. It can be a difficult paradox to deal with. On the one hand, perception hinders what we want most to create; on the other, it promotes the further belief that such a life is impossible to achieve, and so on.

Moving the Stars With Your Words
Harold Davis, Msc.D., Ph.D

We Have the Power

You may not realize it, but nothing is intrinsically beyond your reach—you truly have the Power to experience it all. Again, I speak from personal experience when I tell you with confidence that my life has been a fantastic journey. I wouldn't trade it for anything in the world. Compared to where I started out, it really feels like what I've always wanted.

This is not to say that it has not been one of challenges and unrealized expectations. However, I could never have experienced it without first changing what lay inside me. No change in thinking equals no change in physical life. I needed to give the true vision of my life the energy and focus it deserved. That's how I managed to Move the Stars in my own life.

Here is an example of words you can speak for yourself to stay rooted in the Spiritual Energy Field of All Possibilities (Spirit and Law) regardless of what is happening around you:

> *I realize that I am a very important part of the omnipotent power of Spirit and Law. I am a spirit in the Spirit; I benefit from the flow of pure creative energy in every area of my life. My purpose in life is to receive the support of all the power and knowledge of Spirit.*
>
> *My health, prosperity, and happiness are now being manifested from the perfect consciousness within me. My true goals and dreams are being fulfilled, because Spirit is right where I am.*
>
> *I give thanks for the infinite good and the complete fulfillment of my dreams. I know that Spirit has given me all the gifts of life, and that I have accepted these*

gifts. I know that these gifts are founded on the unconditional love of Spirit with all its wonderful values.

I hereby release the words that I speak into the Universal Mind of Spirit, and in doing so turn the entire responsibility for the manifestation of my life over to the only creative power in the universe.

And so it is...

Speaking these words worked for me, and it will do the same for you, no matter what your starting point or what stars you want to move in your life!

Using the Power

We are to our individual life what Spirit is to the Universe. Every time we speak our words with conviction and faith, we act as the Creative Factor in our lives. The Spiritual Energy Field of All Possibilities (Spirit and Law) plays a similar role in the Universe. The only identifiable difference is where Spirit is Universal and infinite in its capacity. We are specific to our own life. Spirit speaks the Universe into existence, whereas we speak our lives into existence with the help of Spirit.

We are a spirit within the Spirit—the same likeness and quality as the ocean, even if a mere drop in the ocean. Spirit created and continues to create everything in the Universe from itself, and it does so by becoming that thing that it makes. We were made in its likeness; therefore, you are an important part of its creative pattern.

Somehow, we have lost sight of these truths. Organized religion has to some extent, distorted what we truly are. Many local traditions separate us from the truth that might otherwise free us from many problems we have co-created in our personal lives. Understanding these truths would free us to co-create a life that could Move Our Personal Stars.

Understanding the Power

To move the stars in your life, you must understand that you live in the Spiritual Energy Field of All Possibilities (Spirit and Law). This energy field has neither beginning nor end. It is omnipresent, omniscient, and omnipotent. It is the power that moves the cosmic stars. Created in the likeness of Spirit, you have creative power that in turn co-creates with you — whether or not you are fully aware of this gift.

What Restricts the Flow of Our Power?

The Relative Filters that block the flow of creative energy are your past history, the collective unconsciousness, and other present conditions you might be experiencing. These filters work against you when you choose to live your life relative to them. It might be the result of an unconscious choice, made out of ignorance about who you really are. Whatever its origin, these filters are activated every moment you live from the outside in — in other words, object-referring.

The solution is simple: Make a conscious choice that favors living life from the inside out, or real self-referring.

Being the Creative Factor

We co-create our life whenever we say or think I am so-and-so, and then go about filling in the blank.

You might choose to say "I am weak" or "I am strong." You might say "I am sick" or "I am healthy." Whatever you say about yourself is ultimately experienced in the mental and physical universe we all live in. The speed at which this manifestation takes place depends on the Universal Laws, the degree of conviction you have about the words employed, and the level of consciousness at the exact moment you speak.

This is how you can become the Creative Factor in your life and move your stars. It does not matter what your stars are. They can be a health challenge that you want to transcend, a burning desire for abundance, making a difference in the world, or leaving a living legacy. No matter what your stars are, you have the power to move them.

Maximizing Your Star-Moving Power

In order to maximize and focus your ability to move the stars in your life, you must identify completely with Spirit and its Values. That is how you can establish a clear image in your mind's eye of what you—and only you—want to do or have, and you must act in a consistent fashion according to your intuitive promptings. You must recognize who you really are, and after that speak your words as precisely as possible; all the time staying in tune with your intuition as you take inspired mental and physical action. The inspired action you take will cause your stars to move.

Creating Miracles with Your Words: Four Case Studies and a Conclusion

– *William James once said:*
> *Accepting of what has happened is the first step to overcoming the consequences of any misfortune.*

In this book, I have shared the one wisdom I can never part with in my personal life: the tremendous power of words, thoughts, and feelings to alter personal experiences. We literally can direct creative energy into action in such away that changes every aspect of our mental and physical life. Creative energy works under all situations, not just special conditions or special occasions. It works by the Law of Cause and Effects; it is the Law of Mind in Action.

The Law of Cause and Effects works automatically to create your experiences once it receives its instructions. It cannot select or decide; it only knows how to take the action. It is not a respecter of persons. Therefore, all that is required for the Law to work is that our words have intention and desire backed by faith the size of a grain of sand. There is nothing magical about faith. It only allows us to hold to the truth about a situation or condition we would like to experience, long enough for its expression in our mental and physical life.

Moving the Stars With Your Words
Harold Davis, Msc.D., Ph.D

You really can move those stars that show up in your life and those that you truly desire to experience. Imagine yourself at the start of your life, when two cells unite to start a process that lasts approximately 280 days without fail and that takes place every second of everyday. There is power and wisdom that knows how to create every element and every aspect of your life. It is the unfolding of the unseen to the seen.

The amazing thing about this process is that it already knew how to construct your eyes, nose, and fingers. It knew what color your eyes would be and how tall you would finally grow. It knew how to construct your lung in a way that can extract oxygen from the air to redistribute to every cell in your body. Every cell was already aware that the lungs did this, when the process started, and how long the lifetime would last.

My point is this: we are created miraculously yet completely by faith. It should be very easy for us to see the power that created us and continues to give us the gift of life every moment we experience it. We have faith that this process will continue.

This is faith that is larger than a fine grain of sand, and we already possess it. With this awareness, we ought to turn our attention to the invisible essence of our being and realize that it is truly awesome. We should acknowledge that we are part of the same power that courses through us, around us and from us; we should recognize our obvious faith in it.

If you are courageous, willing, loving, and enlightened enough to recognize the truth that surpasses all understanding, the truth will set you free if you get on its side. Then you will move the starts in your life.

Case Studies

So, let me now highlight a few aspects of the philosophy that have benefited the clients I have coached:

CASE ONE

This is an account of the coaching I gave Chaneta Lewis, friend and Inspirational Speaker:

I met Chaneta over nine years ago when she reluctantly attended a business presentation in my home. She was not interested in the opportunity; however, she had a project that she was pursuing named "There For You." She retained me as her Success Coach to help with the project and we have been great friends ever since.

Chaneta is originally from Liberia West Africa, which she and her immediate family had fled after a military dictator took over. They had miraculously escaped what appeared to be certain death and came to America to start a new life. Therefore, Chaneta already knew about the power of faith in a Higher Power, and had a star-moving experience that had the makings of a great epic. However, some unseen force was blocking her success and holding her back.

I started coaching Chaneta in various areas of her life, and she responded very well to the concepts I shared with her. We addressed issues like health, wealth, and happiness. She began to realize the truth about herself and became a serious student of Metaphysical Science.

Thanks to my coaching, Chaneta's health showed marked improvement and she was soon succeeding as an entrepreneur. Her company at the time "There For You" hosted my successful television talk show, and as a result, she became a recognized personality and popular talk-show host.

Moving the Stars With Your Words
Harold Davis, Msc.D., Ph.D

With my assistance, she developed her speaking style and confidence so well that she became a successful seminar leader. Chaneta is also co-founder of Core Essence with her partner Evelyn Coulson. Core Essence is a successful seminar company dedicated to helping people reach their true potential.

Chaneta's Testimony:

Hiring Harold as my success coach was the best thing that ever happened to my life. If you don't know the meaning of coach, look it up before you ask Harold to coach you.

He is relentless! If you want success in life, if you want to see positive, life-changing results, Harold is the person to coach you. He is fearless, dedicated, full of zeal, enthusiastic and caring. He wants you to succeed. He will assist you in accomplishing your goals and living your dreams. That is part of his mission — namely, "positively impacting" people's lives.

When I met Harold, my life was going nowhere. I talked about wanting success, but I didn't know how to go about getting there. Being multitalented, I didn't know what to focus on. Harold took me step by step to find my PASSION, and once I identified it, he coached me to success.

Here is how he did it:

He helped me identify what was holding me back.

He showed me how to overcome my fears and my feeling of helplessness.

He inspired me to take responsibility for my life.

He inspired me to write my vision and mission statements.

He inspired me to write down my goals, plan of action, and timelines.

He helped me to reach deep down inside and bring out all my God-given power.

He provided weekly inspirational coaching sessions.

He helped me get out of my "comfort" zone.

He encouraged me each step of the way; and the list goes on.

Harold never stops until you've reached the goals you say you want! Not only does he coach for success, he lives success. He is a man of his "word" and a man of consistent, congruent action. He is compassionate, understanding, but focused and determined to help you live on purpose and achieve the success you say you want.

This is why today I can confidently say that the turning point in my life for positive change was the day I was blessed to have met my coach, Harold Davis. He helped me Move the Stars in my life.

Chaneta Lewis
Success Coach / Inspirational Speaker / Co founder of Core Essence

CASE TWO

Following is my account of coaching an advance student in health psychology, whom I will call Frank:

Frank was successful in certain aspects of his life, but he was not living up to his true potential. He was working full time and pursuing an advance degree in health psychology. Frank was limiting himself because of a poverty consciousness that created limiting beliefs.

I worked with him for over a year to help him discover the truth about himself, helping him start looking at himself as primarily a spiritual being. This helped Frank raise his prosperity consciousness, which in turn allowed him to challenge the limiting beliefs that had a strong hold on his level of consciousness.

Thanks to my coaching, he started implementing strategies in his life that enabled him to maximize his financial resources and live a better lifestyle.

I cannot say that Frank has fully adopted all the principles I teach—such as Unconditional Love— or that he has fully accepted that he is primarily a spiritual being having human experience. However, I believe he has the potential for a breakthrough because of his exposure to these concepts. We are all at different levels along the journey call life.

Frank's Testimony:

I have had the opportunity to experience Harold's advanced skills in success coaching, I have been able to remove personal obstacles and improve the quality of my life and that of my children's lives. Harold showed me the "illusions" that needed to be transformed in my life.

Since I learned to change my thinking, a path is now open toward financial freedom.

    Frank
    Advance Student

CASE THREE

Following is my account of coaching my good friend René Dickerson to help her find her passion and to re-invent herself with purpose:

When I first met René, she was going through a transition in her life. She had lost sight of her purpose in life. She gave up on her personal goals and career, all because of her mother's illness. She lost sight of the truth about life and about herself, and was not living up to her true potential. The situation in her personal life was causing a life-altering experience.

She decided to hire me as her life coach, and I worked to assist her in discovering the truth about herself and how to live her life from the inside out (real self-referring). With the help of this new awareness, René started seeing life from a brand new perspective that inspired her to re-invent herself. She was able to transcend her personal challenges and transform them by reframing their meaning. She is now helping people from all occupations to accomplish their dreams. She is the founder of Healthy Balance Now, a company dedicated to teaching and sharing winning patterns that are design to help people live a balanced life.

René's Testimony:

Life admits of no accidents. Everything happens for the highest good. In 1998, I received news that would irreversibly change my personal and business life. Doctors diagnosed my mother with ovarian cancer; she had two to three months left to live. Because I had been working in the medical profession as RN, I fully understood the seriousness of her condition. Her doctors told me that I should prepare for a dramatic "transition."

Still, I refused to believe they had all the answers, and that seemed to challenge my medical training. I decided to go against the grain—against just observing, doing, and listening to what the doctors said. I started questioning why it was happening to my mother, and my family, and why my career, personal happiness and life in general felt out of balance.

Moving the Stars With Your Words
Harold Davis, Msc.D., Ph.D

I started to see life as a precious gift, and as a result, my own life began to change for the better. The impact of my mother's condition was leading me on a spiritual, emotional and physical journey. I was ready to learn the truth about myself. That was when Harold Davis appeared in my life.

Harold, my Life Coach, not only taught me the truth about myself, but did it by showing me what potential lay within me.

You can do the same. You may be a successful daughter, businessperson, or community advocate living your own human experience. Harold showed me that I was also a spiritual being. The words he spoke taught me that all my greatness and power lay within me, not outside me.

Once I understood this, the rest was almost effortless. I was able to co-create my life. My stars started to line up. Opportunities graciously began to present themselves. I manifested an abundance of health, wealth, peace, and joy.

Today, I can honestly say that I'm living my dreams, and creating new ones every day. I expect miracles in my life; they are no longer beyond reach. The oddest thing is that I'm not the only person to benefit from these things. I speak and work with others daily, inspiring them to seek a balanced life for themselves.

Perhaps the most wonderful part of life is to know that Harold Davis is a courageous, truthful, inspired, committed leader who talks and walks a life divinely created by God.

René Dickerson
RN / Success Coach, and founder of Healthy Balance Now

Case Study 4

We are never too young or old to live our dream by the power of our words. The Following is my account of coaching Harold Davis, Jr., my son:

My son came to live with me in the summer of the year 2001. He has always been a very good person; however, well-intentioned people in his life seemed to be holding him back. They viewed him as a young boy that had no capacity to know who he wanted to be and what he wanted in life. It might have been their desire to prolong the joys of his childhood, but it was clearly not working for him.

Thirteen years old at the time, Harold showed enough courage to ask if he could move to California and live with me. We always had a great relationship, even though he had not live with me for more than seven years. He asked me to help him grow into his role as a young man and I was delighted to accept this important responsibility. In fact, I had been silently speaking this very situation into existence for a number of years.

Several conditions were keeping Harold from demonstrating his potential. The first was other people's misguided attitude about him. He was sickly and suffering from poor health; he read at a lower grade level, and lacked confidence in himself.

Over the course of two year, I had conversations with him that completely turned his life toward the affirmative. He had a head start on many of my philosophical principles, which I shared with him because he attended numerous functions where I was the Keynote speaker. In retrospect, this exposed him to the whole concept of Metaphysical Science and made it easier to communicate with him at a deeper level.

In less than five month, Harold made a quantum leap, and continued to improve daily. He no longer needed the

Moving the Stars With Your Words
Harold Davis, Msc.D., Ph.D

support of the medication that his mother had been sending; he started reading at his proper grade level; he became the fastest mile runner in his school and holds the record for the fastest recorded time there. Most importantly, he discovered his real self. The result of this amazing turnaround has inspired and empowered him to write a book and to be an inspirational speaker. He has a strong message that everyday inspires me.

Harold's Testimony:

My father is truly an amazing person, he has helped me realize and tap into my true potential and by doing so allowed me to reach out and become aware of new and higher levels of consciousness.

Through my experience of just living with my father, I have learned to let go of the illusions and reach inside of myself to find out the truth about myself. My father has made a positive impact in my life!

There was a time when I was sickly and doubtful, but once I began to open my mind and heart to my father's knowledge, I started to realize that I was born perfect and that I am a perfect child of the living spirit. The knowledge that Dad has taught me and is continuing to share with me is life changing, and I believe that he is making a difference with everyone he meets.

Harold Davis Jr.
Student / Inspirational Speaker / Writer

*   *   *

These four inspiring cases demonstrate how ordinary people from different occupations can transform their lives through their own words, thoughts, and feelings enough to Move their personal Stars. I have coached people with pressing health challenges, financial pressures, and other major concerns centered on some unresolved personal issue. You don't need your back against the wall or be down on your luck before you can benefit from this philosophy. All you need is a positive vision for your life. You have already received your gifts from the Spiritual Energy Field of All Possibilities (Spirit and Law), which has given you dominion over your life. You can co-create the life you deserve, and you deserve to experience it all.

Remember that you, no less than anyone else, have the right and capacity to protect yourself from the pitfalls of your physical environment and to change your present conditions right now. You alone can clear the path in your life and resolve difficult obstacles; you can co-create a life of supreme service for yourself and for others that is worth living. None of us is unique in respect of what we deserve to experience. We all deserve to experience joy and happiness, and this is why our Creator has given us the power to Move the Stars in our lives.

Moving Your Stars

Armed with the awareness of your awesome internal power, imagine another clear night when the stars are extra bright. This time, however, look into the vastness of your creative mind, while being in perfect harmony with Spirit, and speak:
"**Move, Stars!**"

Moving the Stars With Your Words
Harold Davis, Msc.D., Ph.D

Wait patiently and things will start to happen for you. Your prosperity begins to improve, your health is stronger and vibrant, and you feel fulfilled in your life because of your new experiences. You realize that you are the Creative Factor in your life, and that what you are capable of doing as a spiritual being is truly incredible.

You clearly see that you have a power that flows through you, around you, and from you, and that this power has neither beginning nor end.

You realize that it is everywhere present; that it is all the knowledge and power there is; that you are within this power and a vital part of it; therefore, you have the power to move the stars in your life. And as a result of this revelation the stars begin to move for you…

Notes

I Would Like To Hear Your Success Stories!

Send me an e-mail, and tell me about your star moving experiences.

drhdavis@movingthestars.com

The Laws and Principles shared in this book will help you if you apply them to your life and business. I am available to help you reach your potential.

If you are ready to experience the life you deserve, you can call me for a free consultation at (866)200-5174. And discover how you could benefit from my Holistic Coaching Services.

If you would like me to deliver a high-energy keynote or conduct one of my life changing seminars for your large or small group, contact me at:

Moving The Stars Seminars, Inc.
237 Tramway Dr, Suite B, Box 4470
Lake Tahoe, NV 89449
(775)588-6418
(866)200-5174
E-mail: mts@movingthestars.com
Web site: www.MovingTheStars.com

ISBN 141202772-1

9 781412 027724